TRICK
GEOGRAPHY®

THE AMERICAS AND OCEANIA
STUDENT BOOK

Patty Blackmer

Blackmer Press
Walled Lake, MI

Patty Blackmer holds a Bachelor of Arts degree in English and American Language and Literature and a Master of Arts degree in Secondary School Curriculum with an emphasis in linguistics from Eastern Michigan University. She has taught in both public and private schools. Patty and her husband, Ron, have homeschooled their three sons.

Trick Geography
4425 Newton Rd.
Walled Lake, MI 48390
TrickGeography@outlook.com

Visit our website at:
TrickGeography.com

Thank You!

*Ron and our boys Brendan, Colin, and Grant for years of answering my endless requests
for their opinions;*

*Kate Quinlan for her encouraging words, constructive suggestions,
and for piloting the program;*

*Ellyn Davis at HomeSchoolMarketplace.com for her invaluable advice
on publishing and marketing;*

*Tim and Holly Cheyne for their optimism, editing and technical help,
and for getting me across the finish line.*

The Lord bestows on all his own gifts as he doth choose.
It's mine to map his whirling globe and yours to be amused.

P. B.

CONTENTS

You can never cross the ocean until you have courage to lose sight of the shore.

—Christopher Columbus

THE WORLD

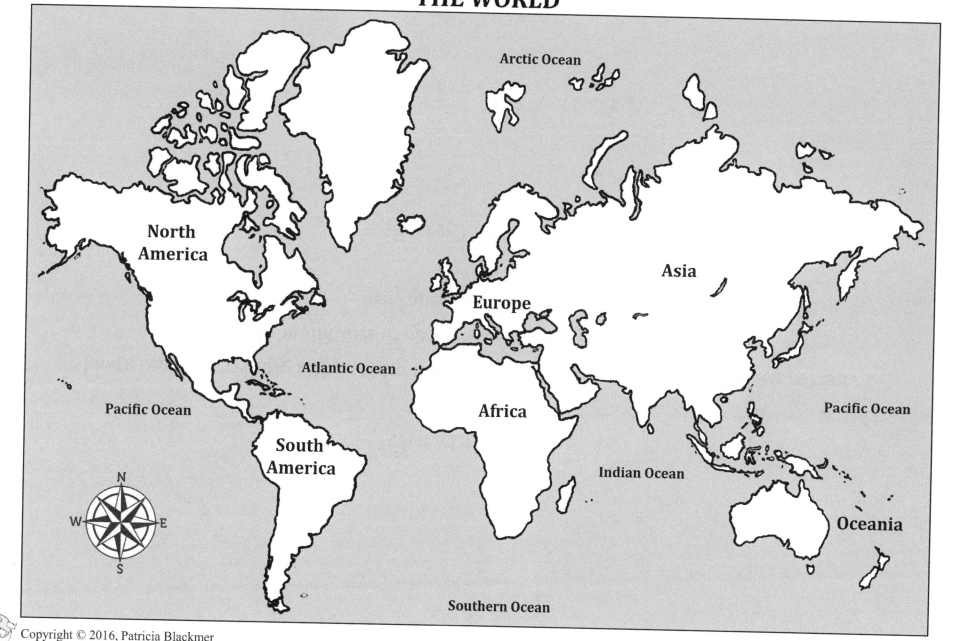

Arctic Ocean

North America

Asia

Europe

Atlantic Ocean

Africa

Pacific Ocean

Pacific Ocean

South America

Indian Ocean

Oceania

Southern Ocean

Character is power.

I have begun everything with the idea that I could succeed, and I never had much patience
with the multitudes of people who are always ready to explain
why one cannot succeed.

—Booker T. Washington

Unit 1:
NORTH AMERICA

NORTH AMERICAN VOCABULARY

Order of countries and capitals correspond.

COUNTRIES

Map 1: North American
1. Greenland
2. Canada
3.a. United States of America
3.b. Alaska
4. Mexico

Map 2: Canadian

Territories
1. Yukon
2. Northwest Territories
3. Nunavut

Provinces
4. Manitoba
5. Saskatchewan
6. Alberta
7. British Columbia

Map 3: Canadian Provinces
1. Ontario
2. Quebec
3. Newfoundland and Labrador
4. Prince Edward Island
5. Nova Scotia
6. New Brunswick

Map 4: Central American
1. Guatemala
2. Belize
3. Honduras
4. El Salvador
5. Nicaragua
6. Costa Rica
7. Panama

Map 5: Caribbean Islands
1. Bahamas
2. Cuba
3. Jamaica
4. Haiti
5. Dominican Republic
6. Puerto Rico
7. Trinidad and Tobago
8. Antiqua and Barbuda
9. St. Kitts and Nevis
10. Dominica
11. St. Lucia
12. Barbados
13. St. Vincent and Grenadines
14. Grenada

CAPITALS

Map 6: North American
1. Nuuk
2. Ottawa
3. Washington, D.C.
4. Mexico City

Map 7: Canadian

Territories
1. Whitehorse
2. Yellow Knife
3. Iqaluit

Provinces
4. Winnipeg
5. Regina
6. Edmonton
7. Victoria

Map 8: Canadian Provinces
1. Toronto
2. Quebec
3. St. John
4. Charlottetown
5. Halifax
6. Fredericton

Map 9: Central American
1. Guatemala City
2. Belmopan
3. Tegucigalpa
4. San Salvador
5. Managua
6. San Jose
7. Panama City

Map 10: Caribbean Islands
1. Nassau
2. Havana
3. Kingston
4. Port-au-Prince
5. Santo Domingo
6. San Juan
7. Port of Spain
8. St. Johns
9. Basseterre
10. Roseau
11. Castries
12. Bridgetown
13. Kingstown
14. St. Georges

NORTH AMERICAN VOCABULARY

Map 11: Bodies of Water
1. Yukon River
2. Great Bear Lake
3. Great Slave Lake
4. Lake Winnipeg
5. Columbia River
6. Snake River
7. Colorado River
8. Gulf of California
9. Rio Grande River
10. Gulf of Mexico
11. Caribbean Sea
12. Mississippi River
13. Missouri River
14. Ohio River
15. St. Lawrence River
16. Gulf of St. Lawrence
17. Hudson Bay
18. Hudson Strait
19. Lake Superior
20. Lake Michigan
21. Lake Huron
22. Lake Erie
23. Lake Ontario

Map 12: Mountains, Deserts, Plains

Mountains
1. Coastal Mountains
2. Mount Denali (McKinley)
3. Rocky Mountains
4. Sierra Madre Mountains
5. Appalachian Mountains
6. Mount Mitchell

Deserts
7. Great Basin Desert
8. Mojave Desert
9 Sonoran Desert
10. Chihuahuan Desert

Plains
11. Great Plains

NORTH AMERICAN REGIONS

1. North America
2. Canadian provinces
3. Central America
4. Caribbean Islands

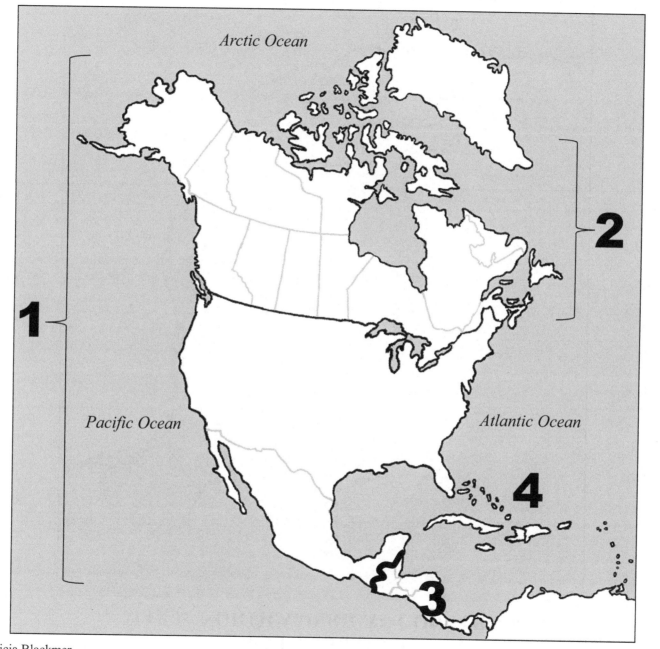

Arctic Ocean

Pacific Ocean

Atlantic Ocean

1

2

3

4

NORTH AMERICA
MAP 1: NORTH AMERICAN COUNTRIES

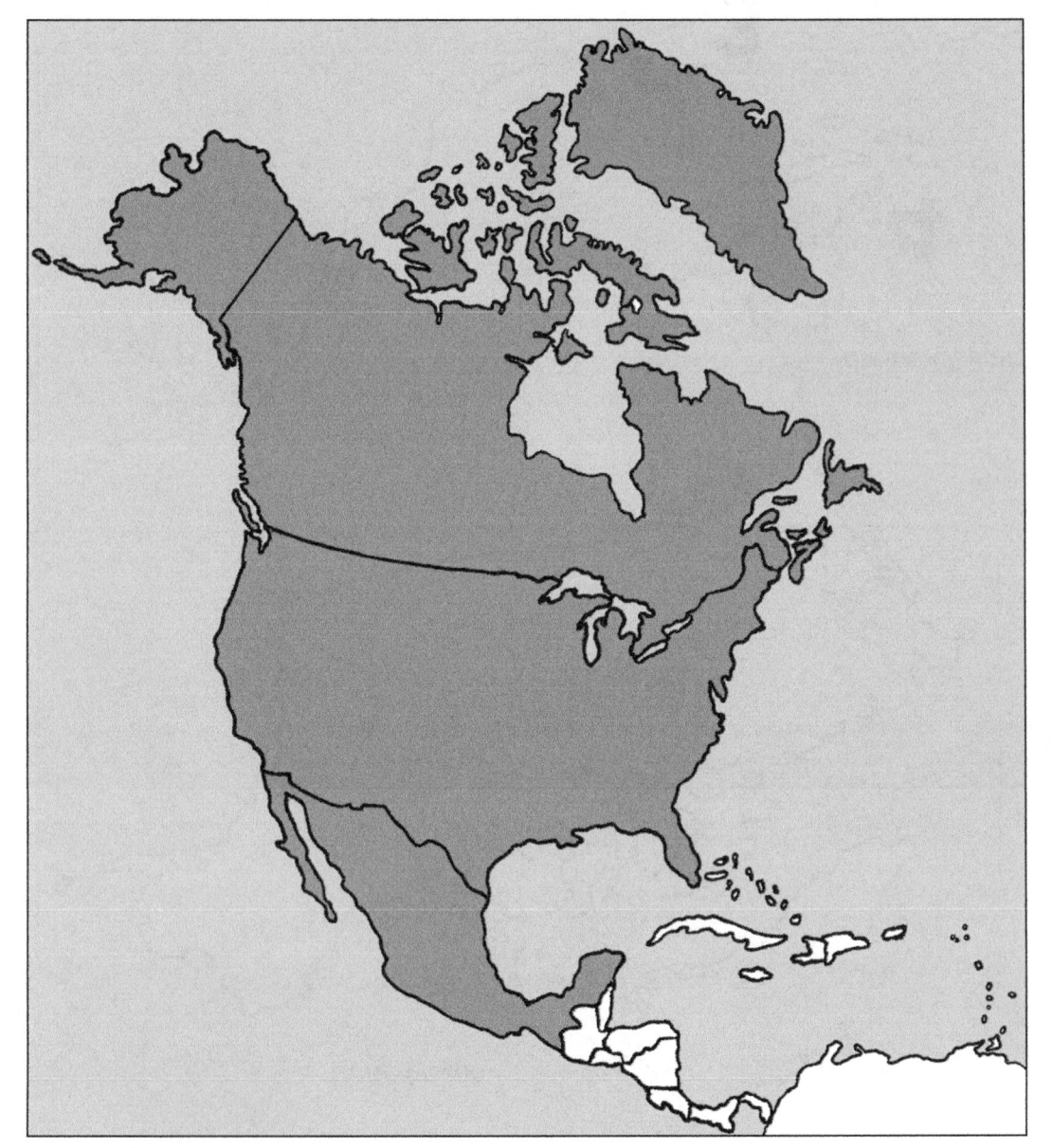

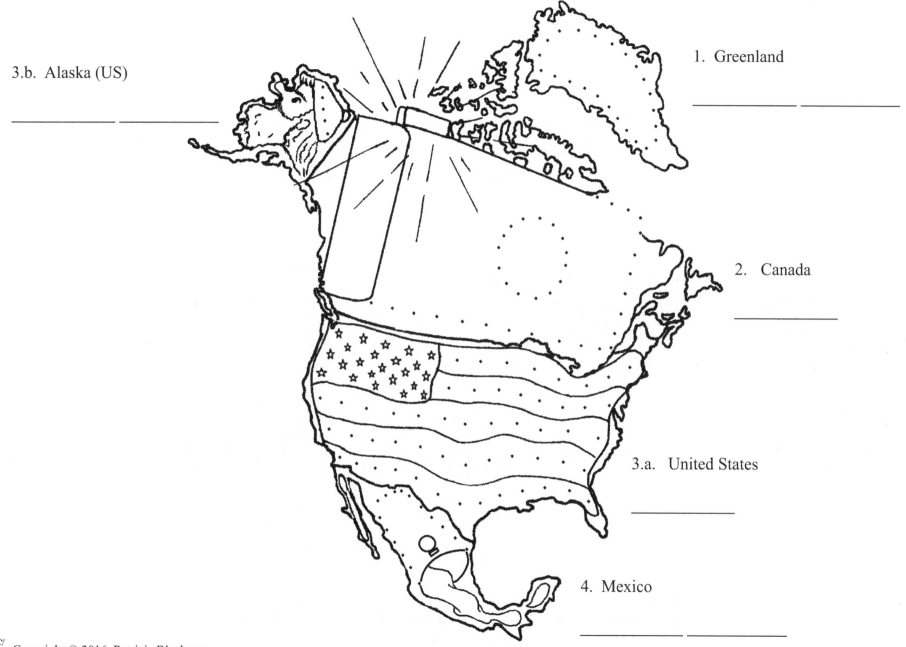

3.b. Alaska (US)

_____ _____

1. Greenland

_____ _____

2. Canada

_____

3.a. United States

_____

4. Mexico

_____ _____

15

NORTH AMERICA
MAP 2: CANADIAN TERRITORIES AND PROVINCES

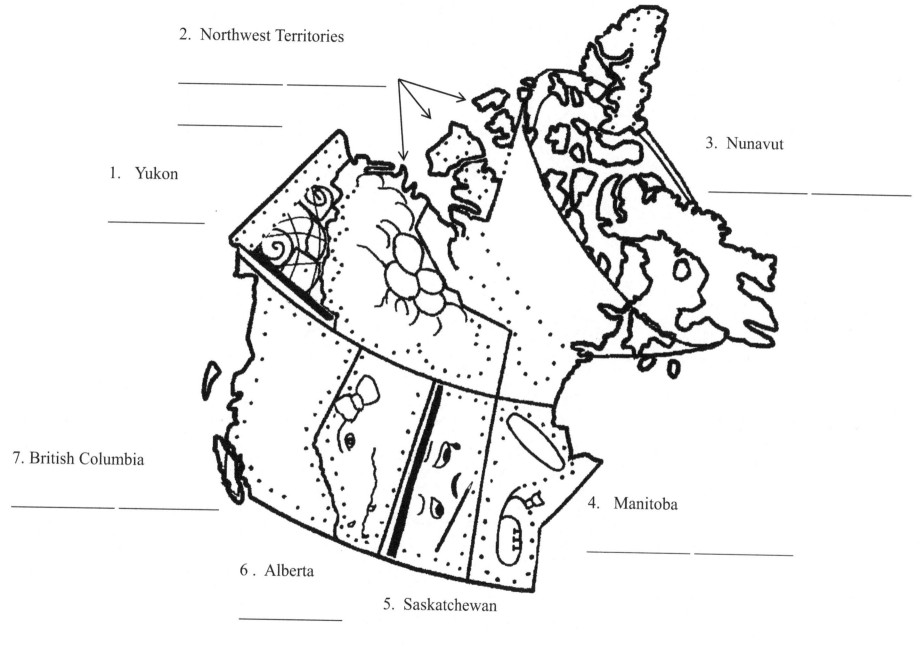

2. Northwest Territories

3. Nunavut

1. Yukon

7. British Columbia

4. Manitoba

6. Alberta

5. Saskatchewan

NORTH AMERICA
MAP 3: CANADIAN PROVINCES

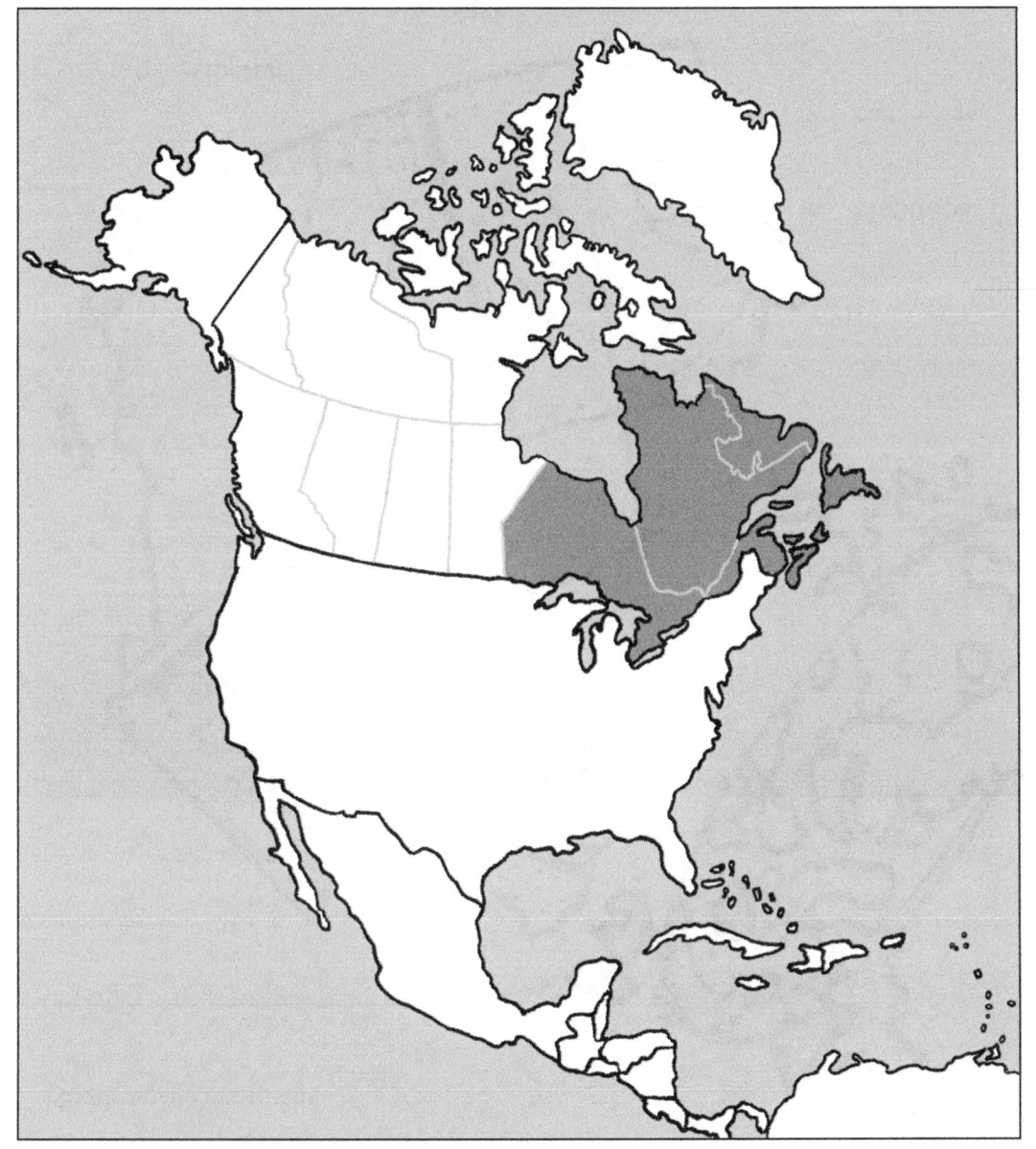

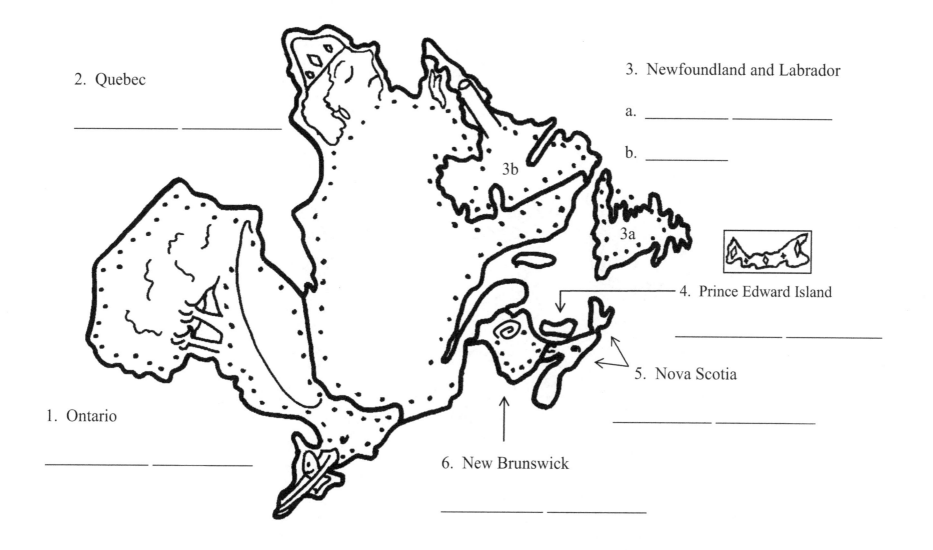

2. Quebec

_____ _____

3. Newfoundland and Labrador

a. _____ _____

b. _____

3b

3a

4. Prince Edward Island

_____ _____

5. Nova Scotia

_____ _____

1. Ontario

_____ _____

6. New Brunswick

_____ _____

NORTH AMERICA
MAP 4: CENTRAL AMERICAN COUNTRIES

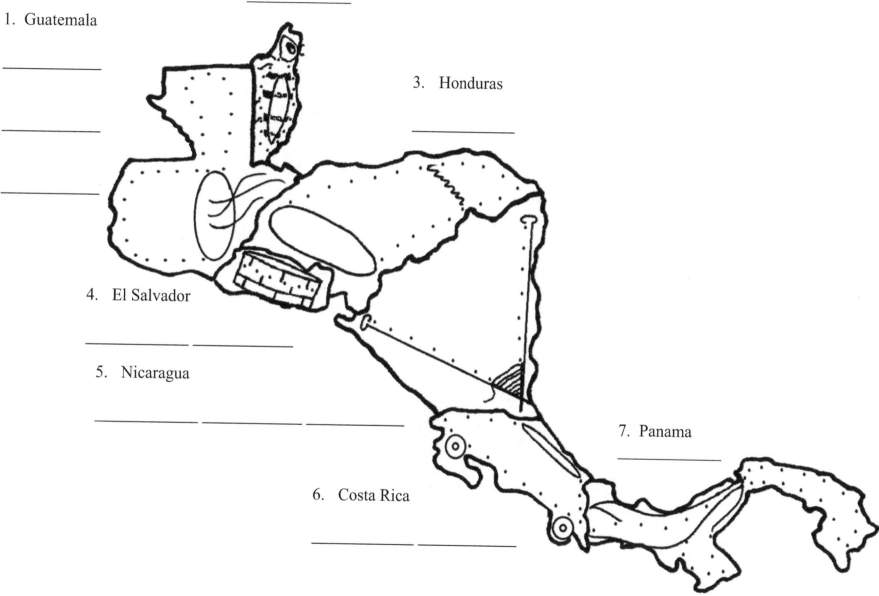

2. Belize

_____

1. Guatemala

_____

_____

_____

3. Honduras

_____

4. El Salvador

_____

5. Nicaragua

_____ _____

_____ _____ _____

7. Panama

_____

6. Costa Rica

_____ _____

NORTH AMERICA
MAP 5: CARRIBEAN ISLAND COUNTRIES

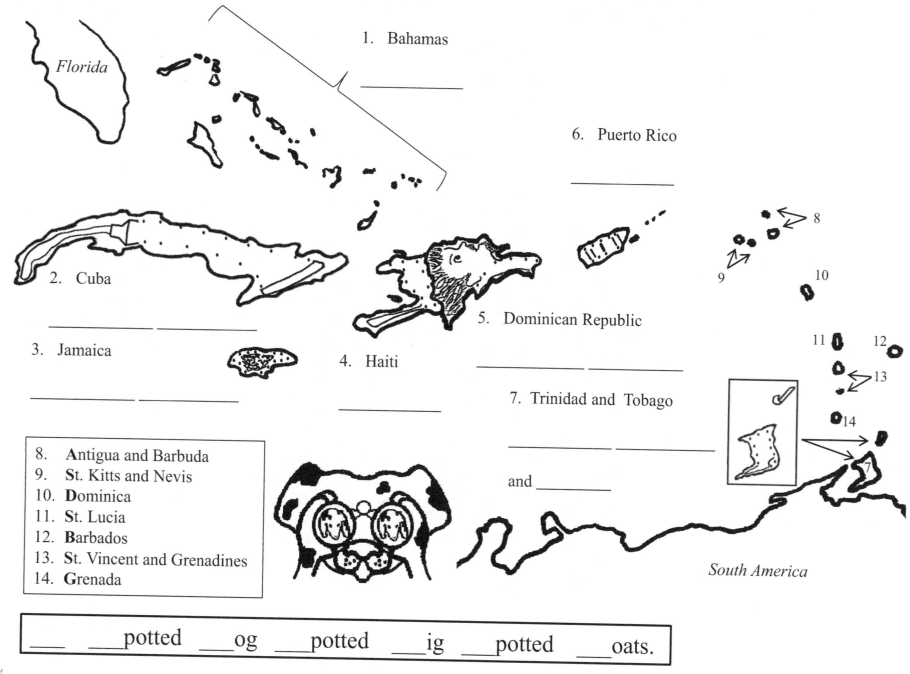

Florida

1. Bahamas

_____

6. Puerto Rico

_____

8

9   10

2. Cuba

_____

3. Jamaica

_____   _____

5. Dominican Republic

_____   _____

4. Haiti

_____

11   12

13

14

7. Trinidad and Tobago

_____   _____

and _____

8. **A**ntigua and Barbuda
9. **St**. Kitts and Nevis
10. **D**ominica
11. **St**. Lucia
12. **B**arbados
13. **St**. Vincent and Grenadines
14. **G**renada

South America

___ ___potted ___og ___potted ___ig ___potted ___oats.

23

NORTH AMERICA
MAP 6: NORTH AMERICAN CAPITALS

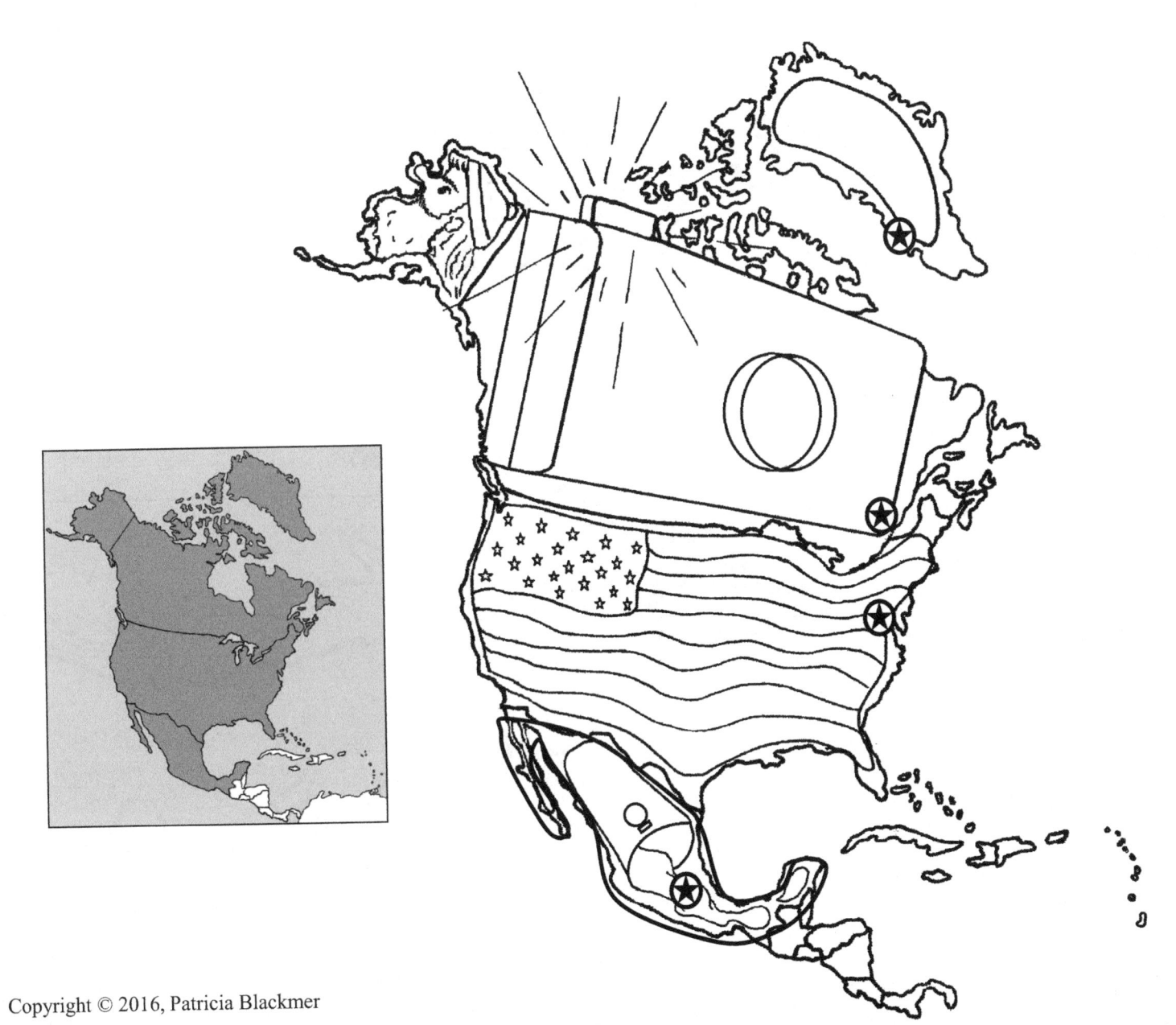

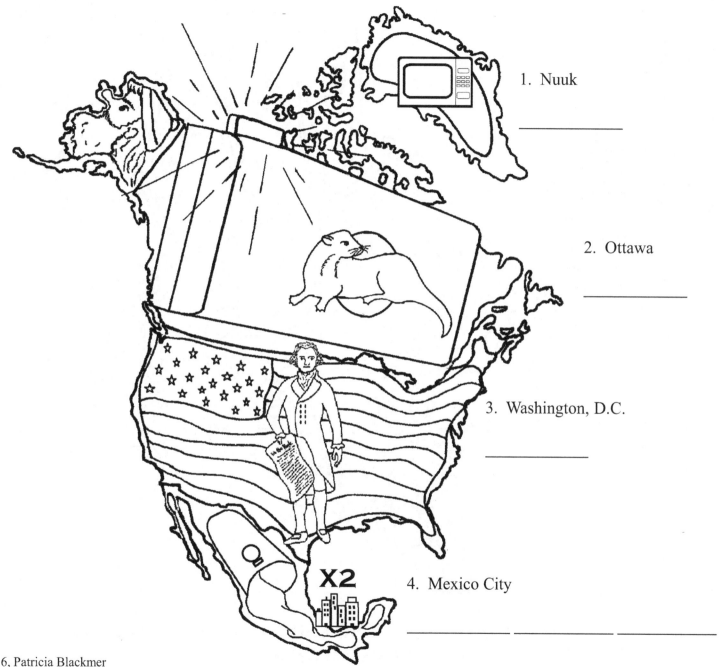

1. Nuuk

_____

2. Ottawa

_____

3. Washington, D.C.

_____

4. Mexico City

_____ _____ _____

NORTH AMERICA
MAP 7: CANADIAN TERRITORY AND PROVINCE CAPITALS

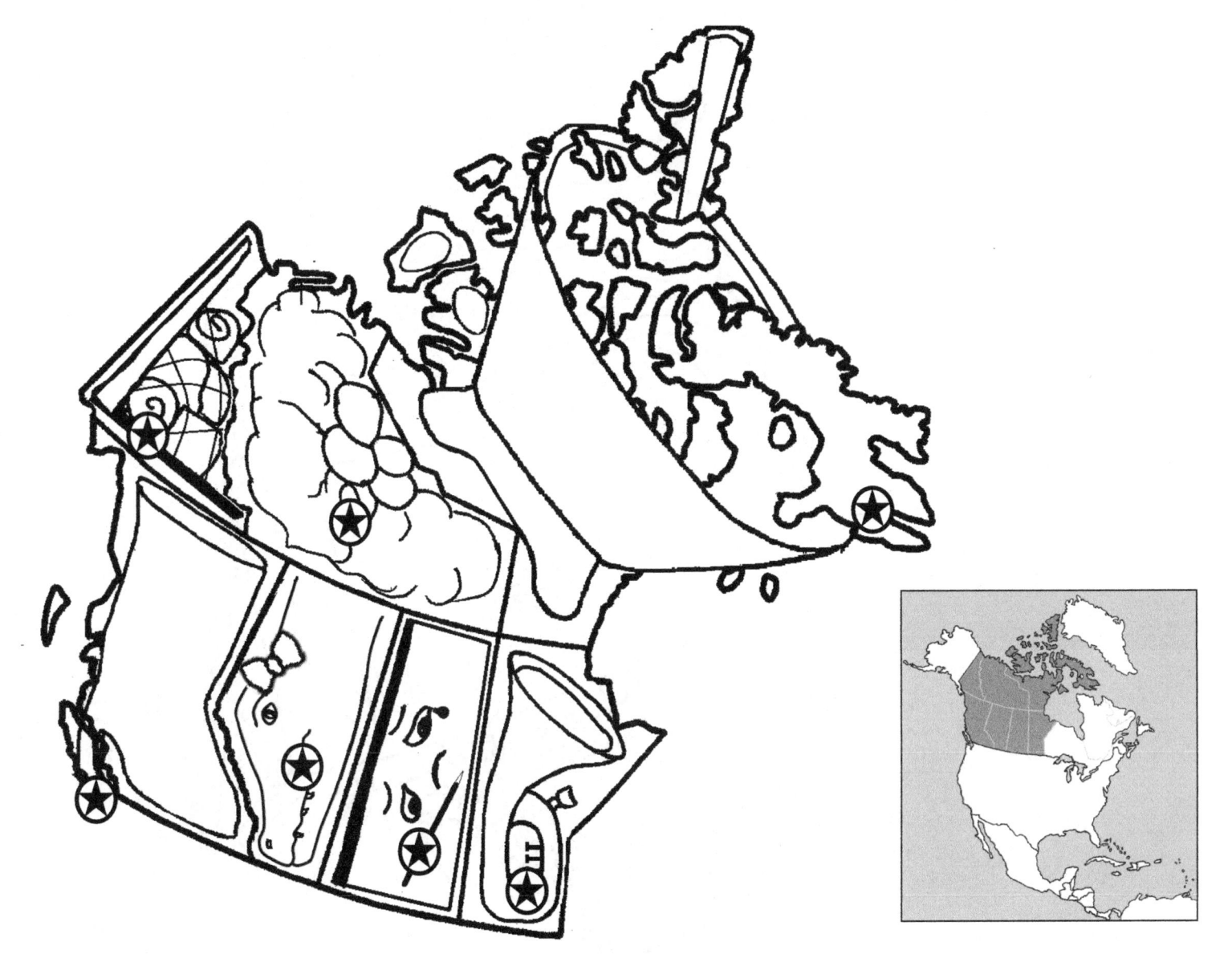

2. Yellow Knife

_____ _____

3. Iqaluit

1. Whitehorse

_____ _____

_____ _____

_____ _____

7. Victoria

_____

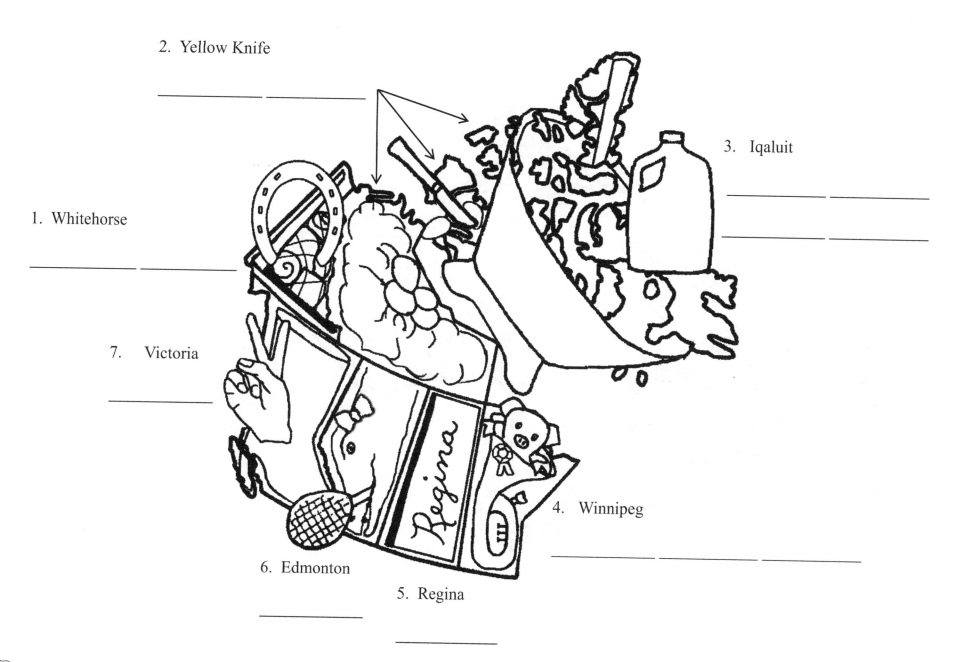

4. Winnipeg

6. Edmonton

_____ _____ _____

5. Regina

_____

_____

NORTH AMERICA
MAP 8: CANADIAN PROVINCE CAPITALS

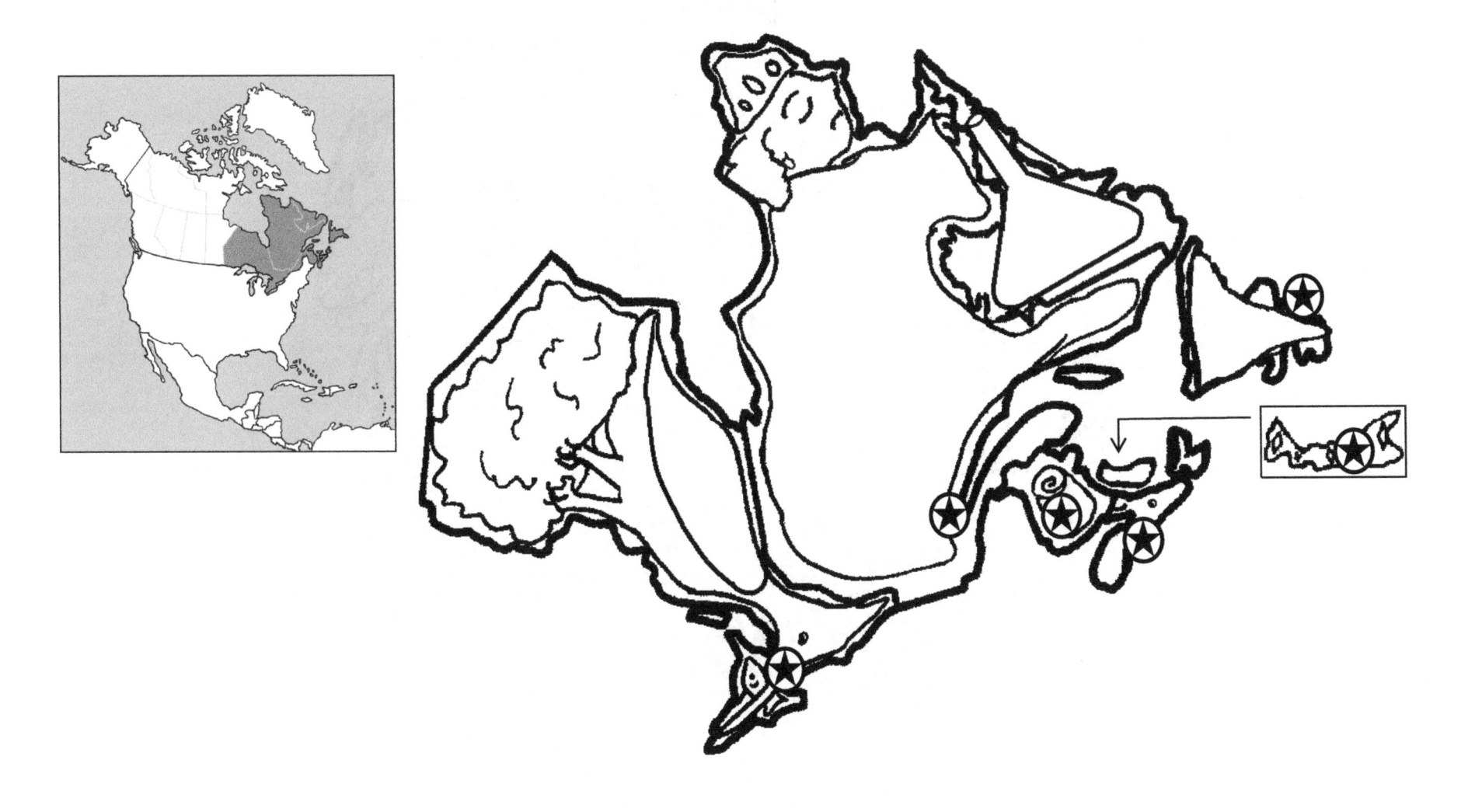

1. Toronto

2. Quebec

3. St. John

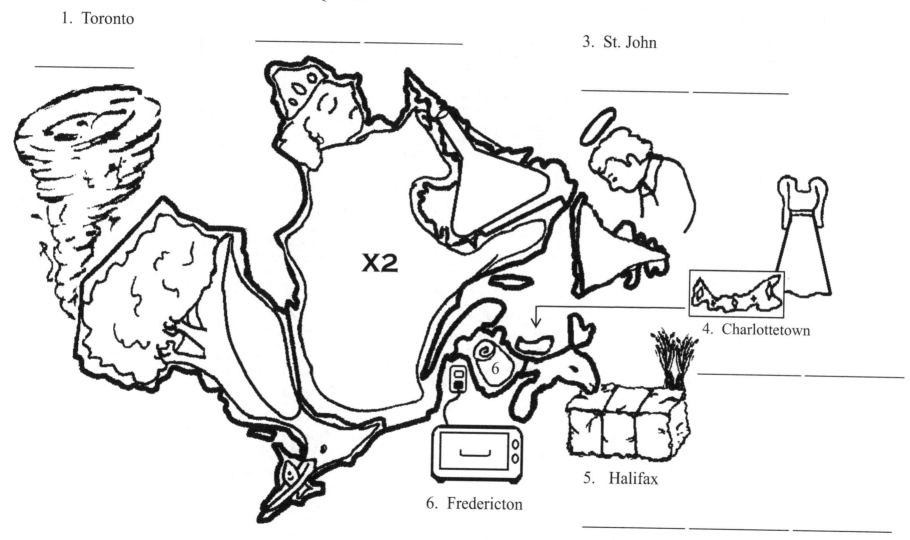

X2

4. Charlottetown

6. Fredericton

5. Halifax

NORTH AMERICA
MAP 9: CENTRAL AMERICAN CAPITALS

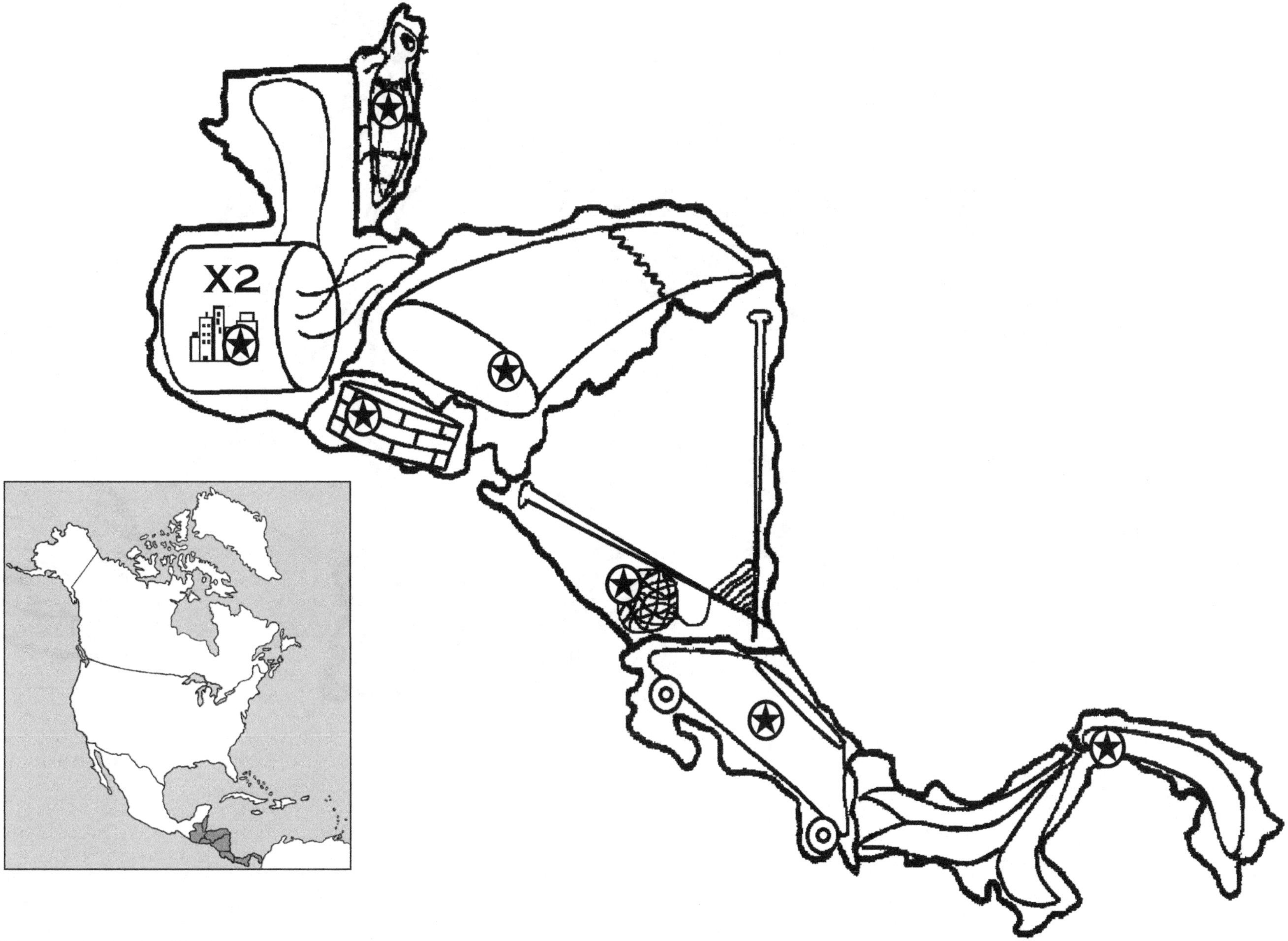

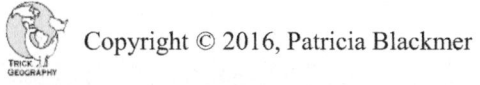

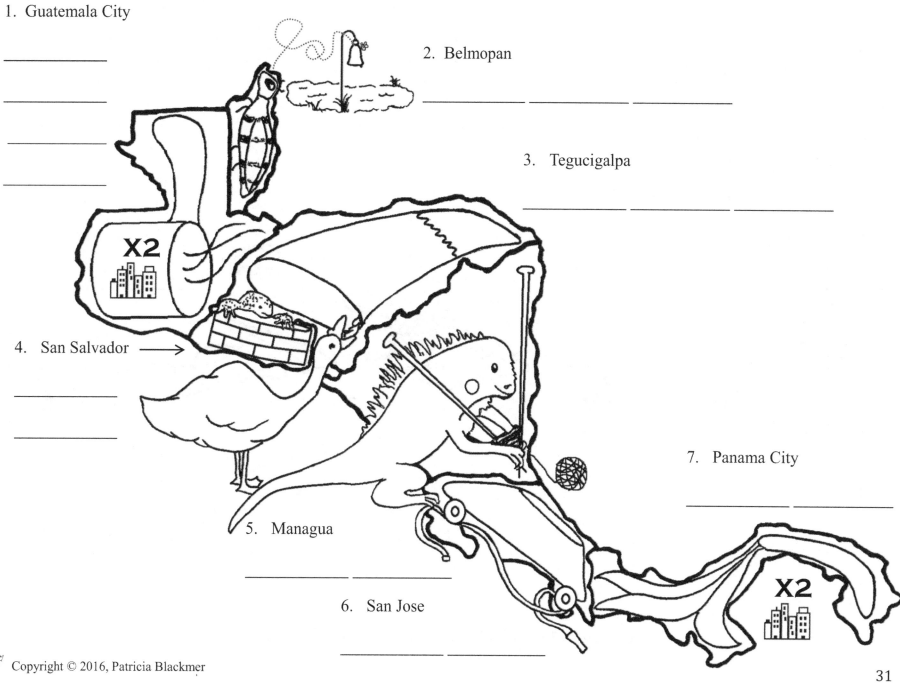

1. Guatemala City

_____

_____

_____

2. Belmopan

_____ _____ _____

3. Tegucigalpa

_____ _____ _____

4. San Salvador →

_____

_____

5. Managua

_____ _____

6. San Jose

_____ _____

7. Panama City

_____

NORTH AMERICA
MAP 10: CARRIBEAN ISLAND CAPITALS

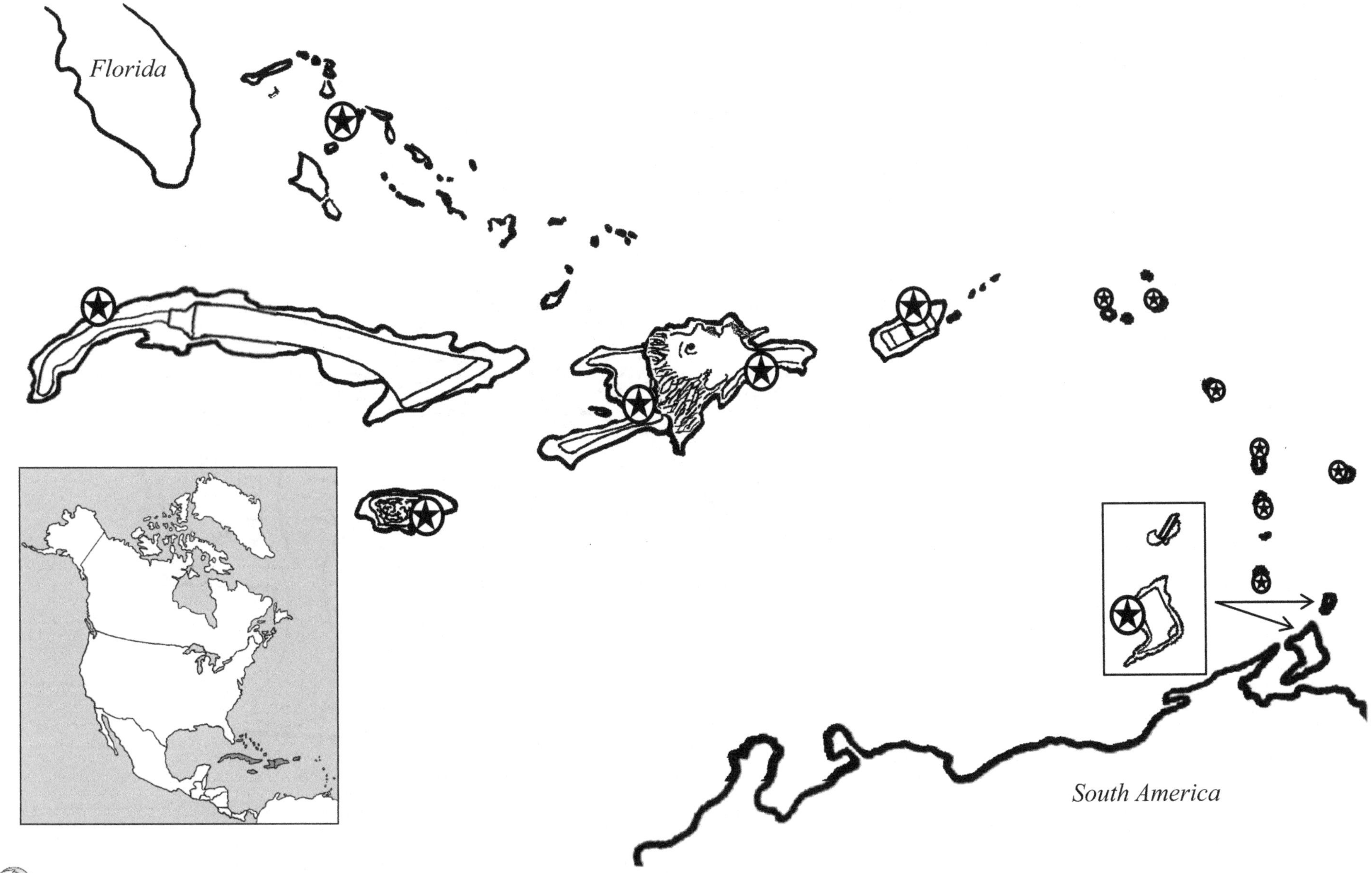

Florida

South America

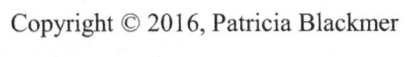

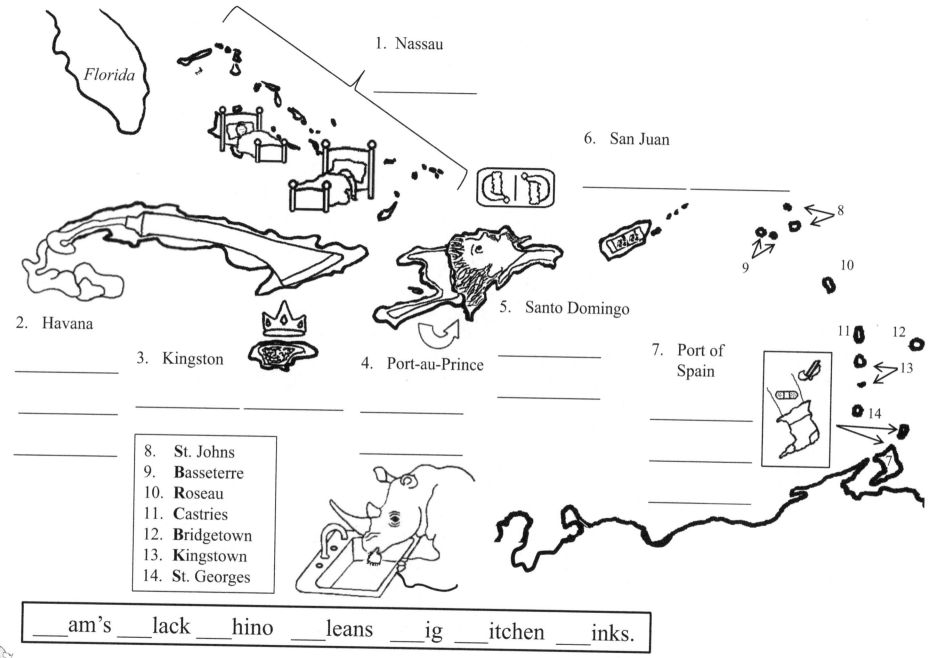

Florida

1. Nassau

6. San Juan

2. Havana

3. Kingston

5. Santo Domingo

4. Port-au-Prince

7. Port of Spain

8
9
10
11
12
13
14

8. **St**. Johns
9. **B**asseterre
10. **R**oseau
11. **C**astries
12. **B**ridgetown
13. **K**ingstown
14. **St**. Georges

___am's ___lack ___hino ___leans ___ig ___itchen ___inks.

33

NORTH AMERICA
MAP 11: BODIES OF WATER

Arctic
Ocean

1

2

3

18

17

5

4

16

5

6

12

15

7

13

14

Pacific Ocean

12

Atlantic Ocean

9

10

8

11

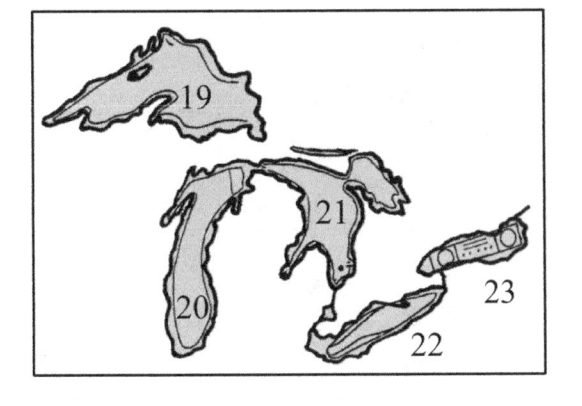

19

21

20

23

22

TRICK GEOGRAPHY

1. **Yukon** River: Flows through _____.

2. **Great Bear** Lake: A _____ big _____ raided the north nest (Northwest Territories).

3. **Great Slave** Lake: A _____ _____ rescued the north nest (Northwest Territories).

4. Lake **Winnipeg**: Lies north of _____.

5. **Columbia** River: Flows through British _____.

6. **Snake** River: The _____ is slithering across the stars on the American flag (USA).

7. **Colorado** River: The American (USA) added food _____ to the mixing bowl (Mexico).

8. Gulf of **California**: Lies south of _____.

9. **Rio Grande** River: It's _____ _____ because it separates two countries.

10. Gulf of **Mexico**: Lies east of _____.

11. **Caribbean** Sea: Dominic the Republican (Dominican Republic) likes _____ and _____.

12. **Mississippi** River: A _____ _____ cup is dripping down the middle of the USA.

13. **Missouri** River: A _____ _____ after the missing sippy cup (Mississippi River).

14. **Ohio** River: _____, _____! We've found the missing sippy cup (Mississippi River).

15. **St. Lawrence** River: _____ _____ put his coat on the ground for Queen Becky (Quebec).

16. Gulf of **St. Lawrence**: _____ _____ still has his coat on the ground for Queen Becky (Quebec).

17. **Hudson** Bay: A hamster named _____.

18. **Hudson Strait**: _____ has his arms out _____.

19. Lake **Superior**: A creature looking for his _____.

20. Lake **Michigan**: The other _____ went through the wash.

21. Lake **Huron**: A _____ _____ the mitten.

22. Lake **Erie**: A rabbit's _____.

23. Lake **Ontario**: The rabbit's ear is listening to a _____.

 Copyright © 2016, Patricia Blackmer

NORTH AMERICA
MAP 12: MOUNTAINS, DESERTS, PLAINS

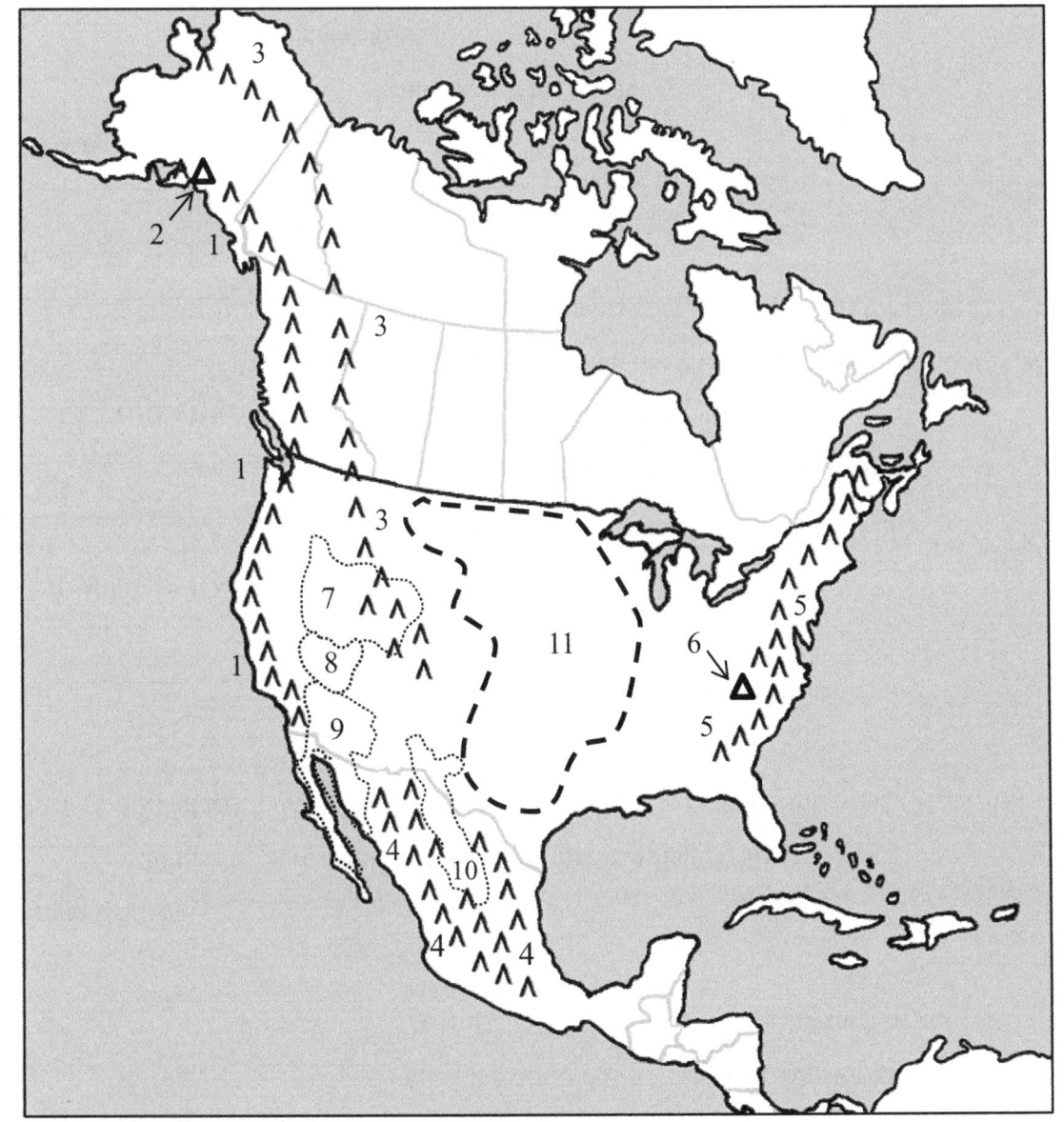

Mountains

1. **Coastal** Mountains: Run along the west _____ of North America.

2. Mount **Denali**: Al asks (Alaska) who gave a _____ to President _____.
   (Mount **McKinley**)

3. **Rocky** Mountains: Al asks (Alaska) to store _____ in the great basin (Great Basin Desert).

4. **Sierra Madre** Mountains: Spanish, the language of _____, for "mother mountain range."

5. **Appalachian** Mountains: The _____ rolled down the east coast.

6. Mount **Mitchell**: _____ bought some apples (Appalachian Mountains).

Deserts

7. **Great Basin** Desert: The _____ _____ has an American flag (USA) engraved on it.

8. **Mojave** Desert: The American (USA) got a _____ haircut.

9. **Sonoran** Desert: The cook stirring the mixing bowl (Mexico) started _____.

10. **Chihuahuan** Desert: The _____ bumped the mixing bowl (Mexico) over.

Plains

11. **Great** Plains: The _____ big _____ landed in the middle of the United States.

If I listen I have the advantage, if I speak others have it.
—Peruvian Proverb

When one is helping another, both gain in strength.
—Ecuadorian Proverb

Unit 2:
SOUTH AMERICA

SOUTH AMERICAN VOCABULARY

Order of countries and capitals correspond.

COUNTRIES   CAPITALS

Map 1: Northeastern
1. Colombia
2. Venezuela
3. Guyana
4. Suriname
5. French Guiana
6. Brazil
7. Uruguay

Map 2: Southwestern
1.a.Ecuador
1.b.Galapagos Islands
2. Peru
3. Bolivia
4. Paraguay
5. Argentina
6. Chile

Map 3: Northeastern
1. Bogota
2. Caracas
3. Georgetown
4. Paramaribo
5. Cayenne
6. Brasilia
7. Montevideo

Map 4: Southwestern
1. Quito
2. Lima
3. La Pas, Sucre
4. Asunción
5. Buenos Aires
6. Santiago

Map 5: Bodies of Water, Mountains

Bodies of Water
1. Orinoco River
2. Amazon River
3. Madeira River
4. Lake Titicaca
5. Paraguay River
6. Paraná River
7. Uruguay River
8. Strait of Magellan

Mountains
9. Andes Mountains
10. Brazilian Highlands

SOUTH AMERICAN REGIONS

1. Northeastern
2. Southwestern

Pacific Ocean

Atlantic Ocean

SOUTH AMERICA
MAP 1: NORTHEASTERN COUNTRIES

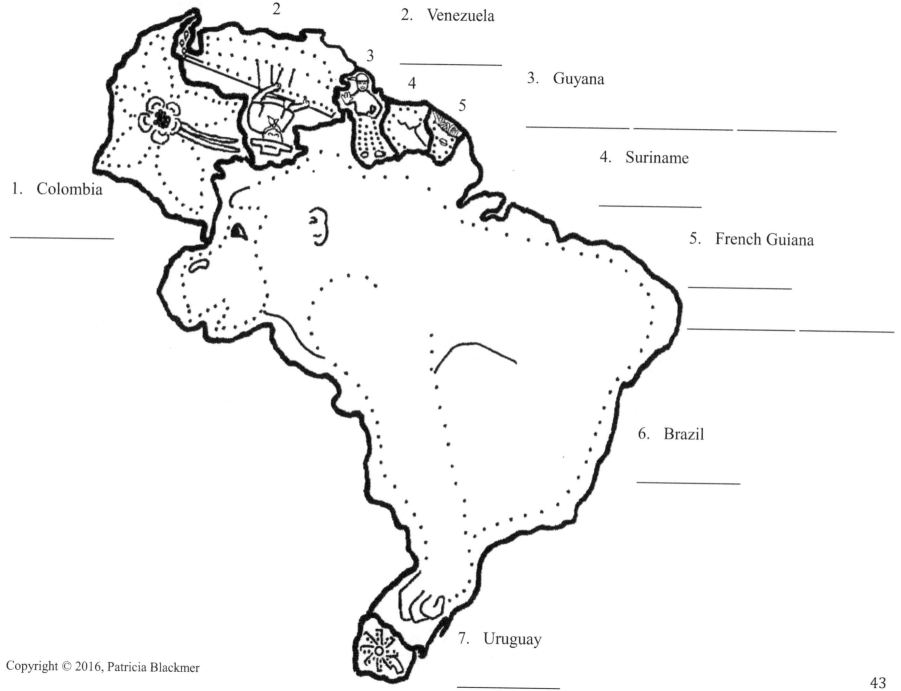

2.   Venezuela

3.   Guyana

4.   Suriname

1.   Colombia

5.   French Guiana

6.   Brazil

7.   Uruguay

SOUTH AMERICA
MAP 2: SOUTHWESTERN COUNTRIES

1. a. Ecuador   ✿ 1.b.

_____ _____

1.b. Galapagos Islands (Ec)

_____

1.a.

2. Peru

_____

3. Bolivia

_____ _____

4. Paraguay

_____ _____

5. Argentina

_____ _____

6. Chile

_____

SOUTH AMERICA
MAP 3: NORTHEASTERN CAPITALS

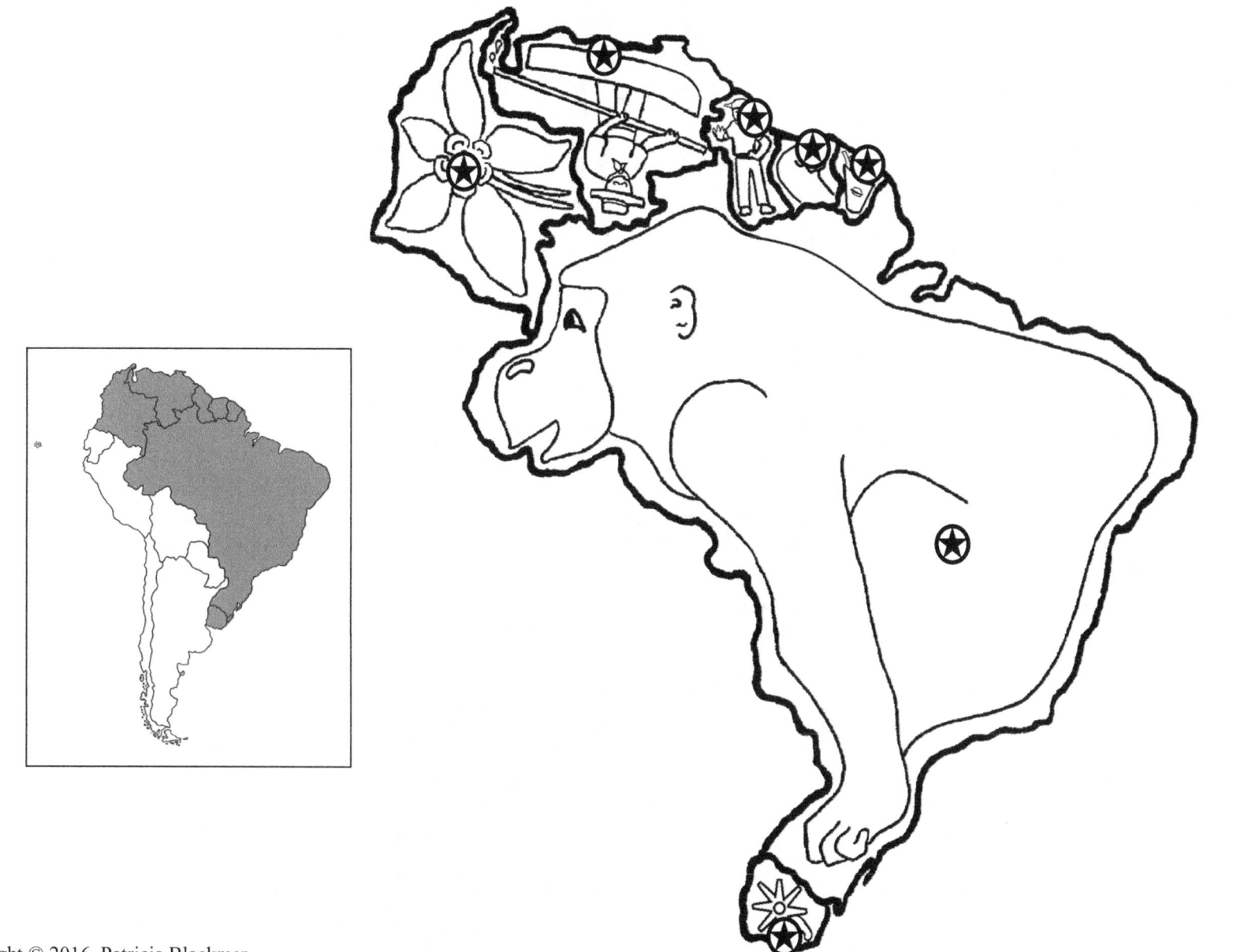

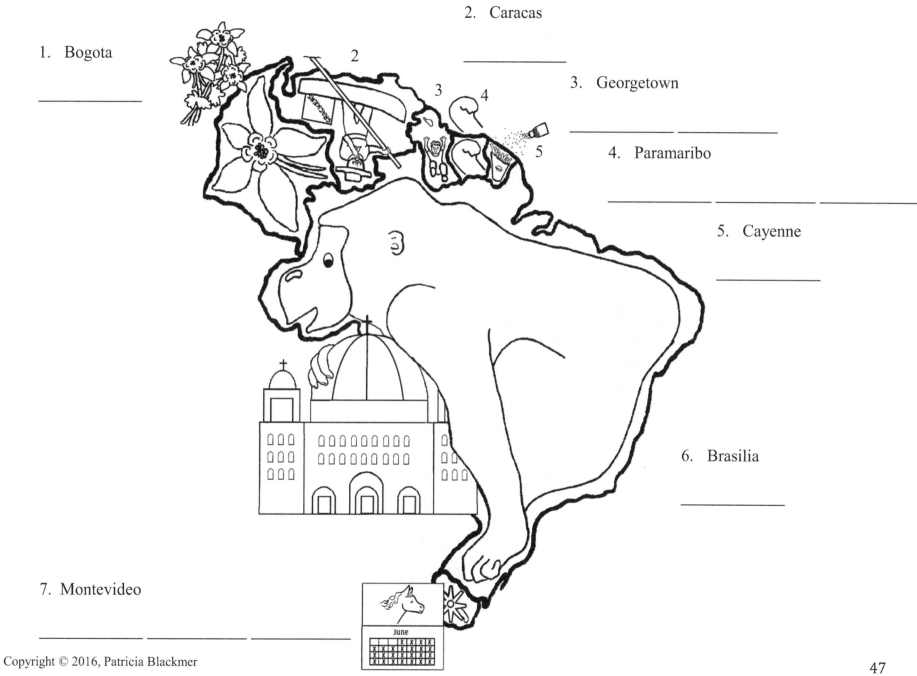

1. Bogota

_____

2. Caracas

_____

3. Georgetown

_____ _____

4. Paramaribo

_____ _____ _____

5. Cayenne

_____

6. Brasilia

_____

7. Montevideo

_____ _____ _____

1. Quito

_____ _____

2. Lima

_____

3. La Pas

_____ _____

Sucre

_____

4. Asuncion

_____ _____

6. Santiago

_____ _____

5. Buenos Aires

_____

SOUTH AMERICA
MAP 5: BODIES OF WATER, MOUNTAINS

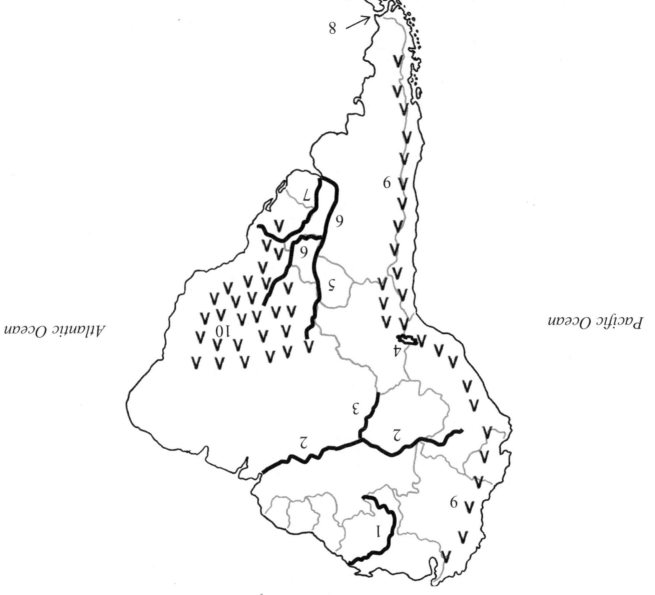

Pacific Ocean

Atlantic Ocean

Bodies of Water

1. **Orinoco** River: The gondolier (Venezuela) puts _____ on his crackers.

2. **Amazon** River: The gorilla (Brazil) is an _____.

3. **Madeira** River: The gorilla (Brazil) is _____ because this river is choking him.

4. Lake **Titicaca**: A cat who purrs (Peru) is a content _____ _____.

5. **Paraguay** River: Cuts _____ in half.

6. **Paraná** River: Arguing Tina (Argentina) saw the _____ bite the gorilla (Brazil).

7. **Uruguay** River: Flows west of _____.

8. Strait of **Magellan**: Arguing Tina (Argentina) ate _____ _____ sandwich.

Mountains

9. **Andes** Mountains: _____ travelled down the west coast of South America.

10. **Brazilian** Highlands: In _____.

Ambition leads me not only farther than any other man has been before me, but as far as I think it possible for man to go.

Do just once what others say you can't do, and you will never pay attention to their imitations again.

—Captain James Cook

Unit 3: OCEANIA

OCEANIC VOCABULARY

Order of countries and capitals correspond.

COUNTRIES

Map 1: Southwestern
1.a. Australia
1.b. Tasmania
2. Papua New Guinea
3. New Zealand

Map 2: Pacific Island Regions
A. Micronesia
B. Melanesia
C. Polynesia

Map 3: Pacific Islands

A. **Micronesian**
1. Palau
2. Federated States of Micronesia
3. Marshall Islands
4. Kiribati
5. Nauru

B. **Melanesian**
6. Solomon Islands
7. Vanuatu
8. Fiji

C. **Polynesian**
9. Tuvalu
10. Samoa
11. Tonga

CAPITALS

Map 4: Southwestern
1. Canberra
2. Port Moresby
3. Wellington

Map 5: Pacific Islands

A. **Micronesian**
1. Ngerulmud
2. Palikir
3. Majuro
4. Tarawa
5. Yaren

B. **Melanesian**
6. Honiara
7. Port-Vila
8. Suva

C. **Polynesian**
9. Funafuti
10. Apia
11. Nukualofa

Map 6: Bodies of Water, Mountains, Deserts, Reef

Bodies of Water
1. Coral Sea
2. Darling River
3. Murray River
4. Tasman Sea

Mountains
5. Great Dividing Range
6. Southern Alps

Deserts
7. Great Sandy Desert
8. Great Victorian Desert

Reef
9. Great Barrier Reef

OCEANIC REGIONS

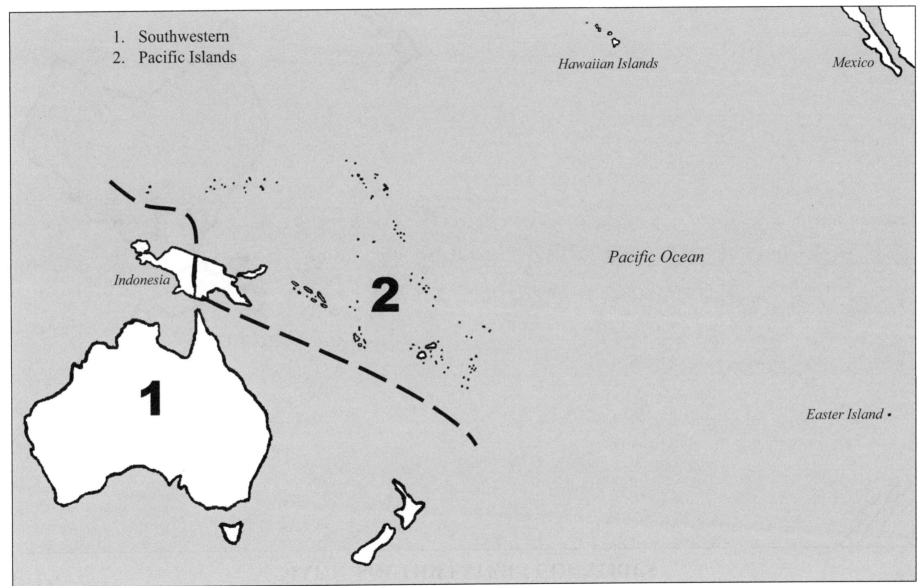

1. Southwestern
2. Pacific Islands

Hawaiian Islands

Mexico

Pacific Ocean

Indonesia

2

1

Easter Island •

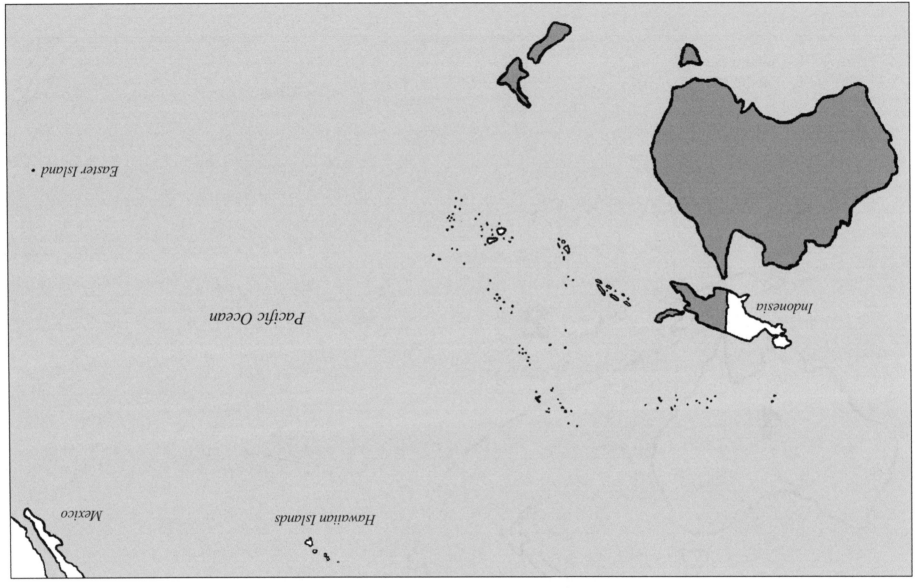

OCEANIA
MAP 1: SOUTHWESTERN COUNTRIES

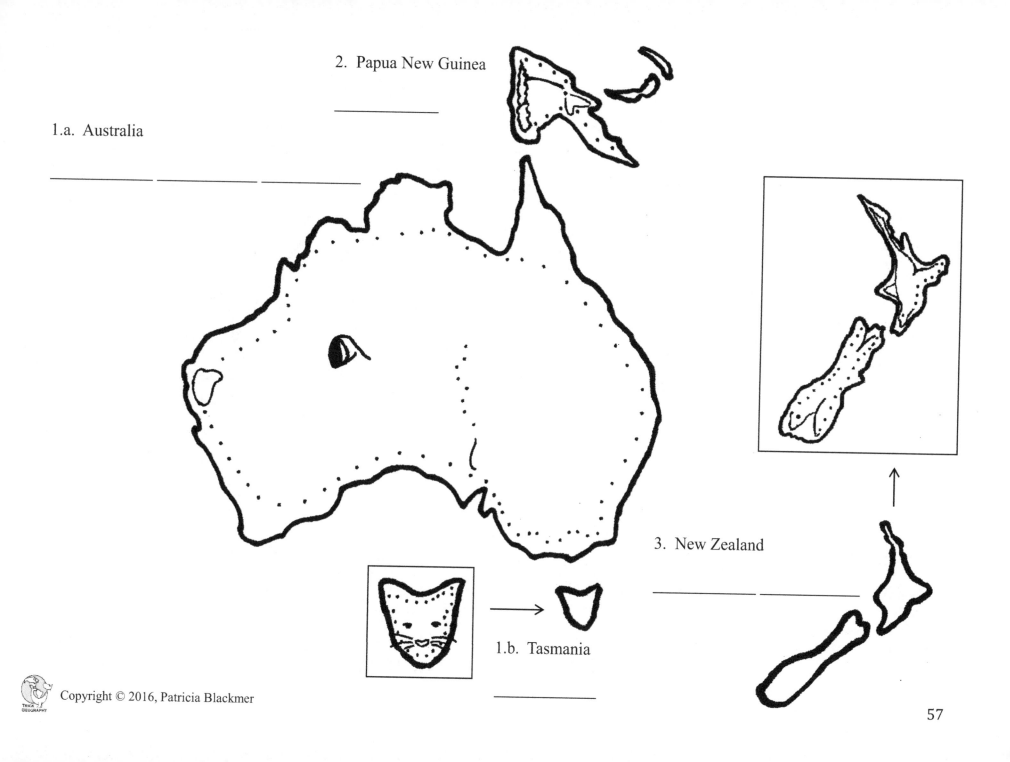

2. Papua New Guinea

_____

1.a. Australia

_____ _____

3. New Zealand

_____

1.b. Tasmania

_____

57

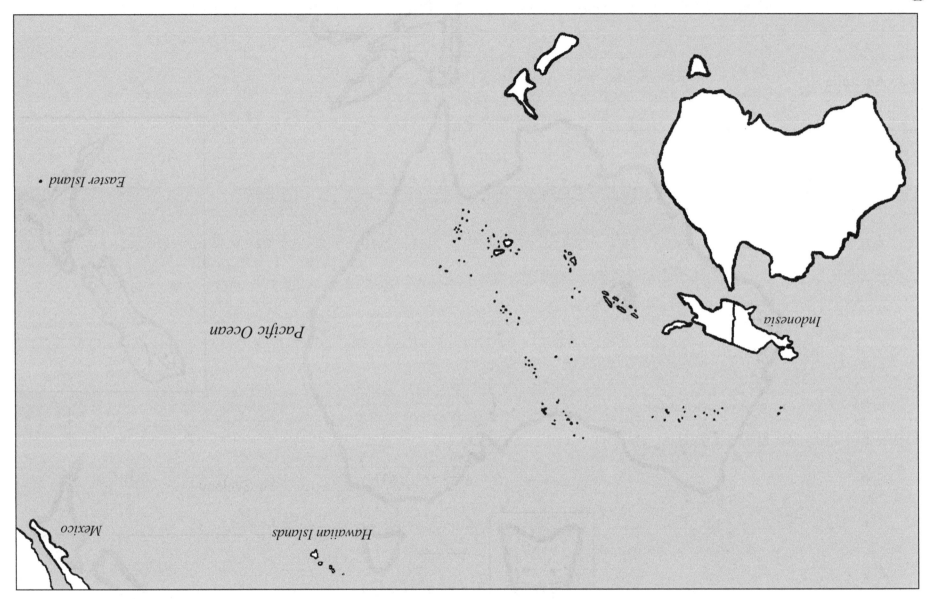

Easter Island

Pacific Ocean

Indonesia

Mexico

Hawaiian Islands

OCEANIA
MAP 2: PACIFIC ISLAND REGIONS

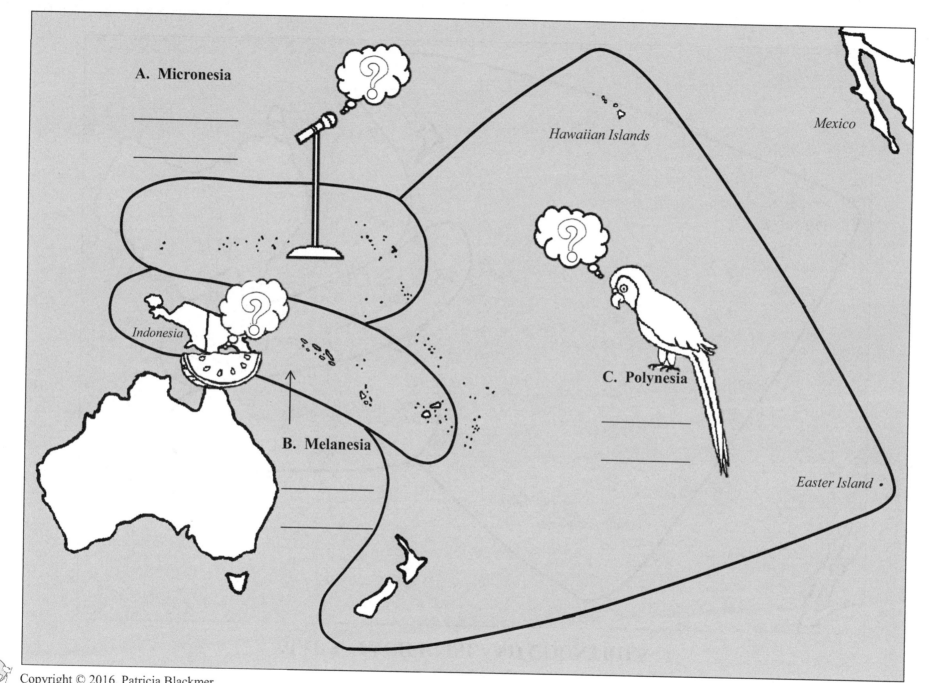

A. Micronesia

_____

_____

Hawaiian Islands

Mexico

Indonesia

B. Melanesia

_____

_____

C. Polynesia

_____

_____

Easter Island

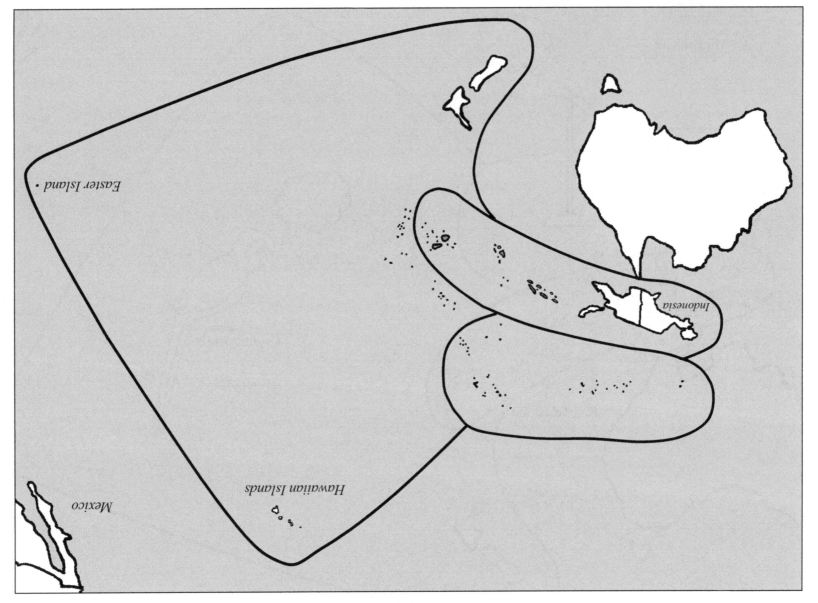

OCEANIA
MAP 3: PACIFIC ISLAND COUNTRIES

Easter Island

Mexico

Hawaiian Islands

Indonesia

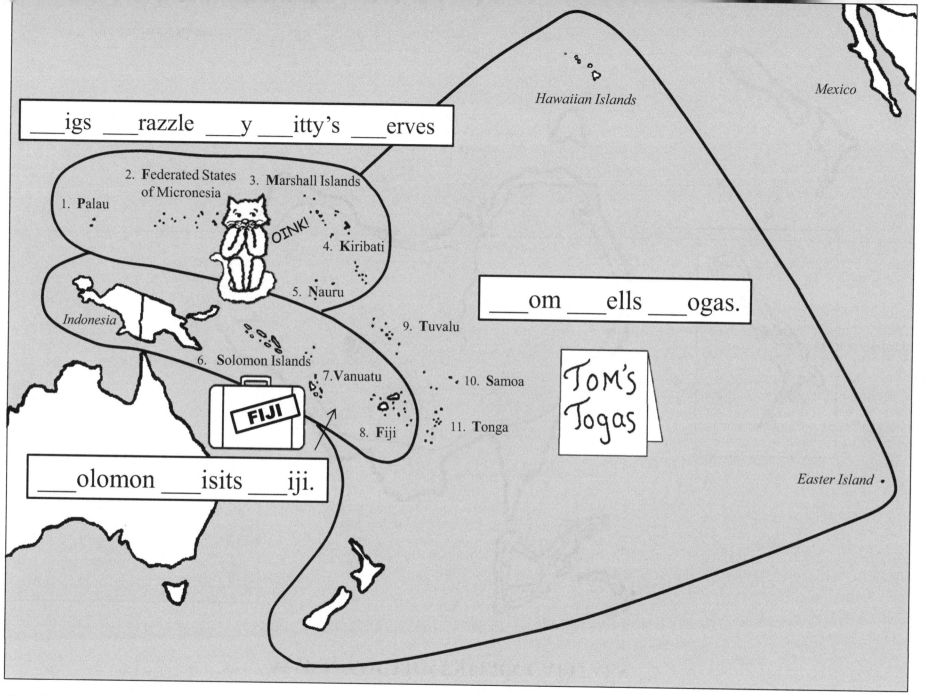

___igs ___razzle ___y ___itty's ___erves

___om ___ells ___ogas.

___olomon ___isits ___iji.

TOM'S TOGAS

1. Palau
2. Federated States of Micronesia
3. Marshall Islands
4. Kiribati
5. Nauru
6. Solomon Islands
7. Vanuatu
8. Fiji
9. Tuvalu
10. Samoa
11. Tonga

OINK!

FIJI

Hawaiian Islands

Mexico

Indonesia

Easter Island

OCEANIA
MAP 4: SOUTHWESTERN CAPITALS

2. Port Moresby

_____ _____ _____

1. Canberra

_____

3. Wellington

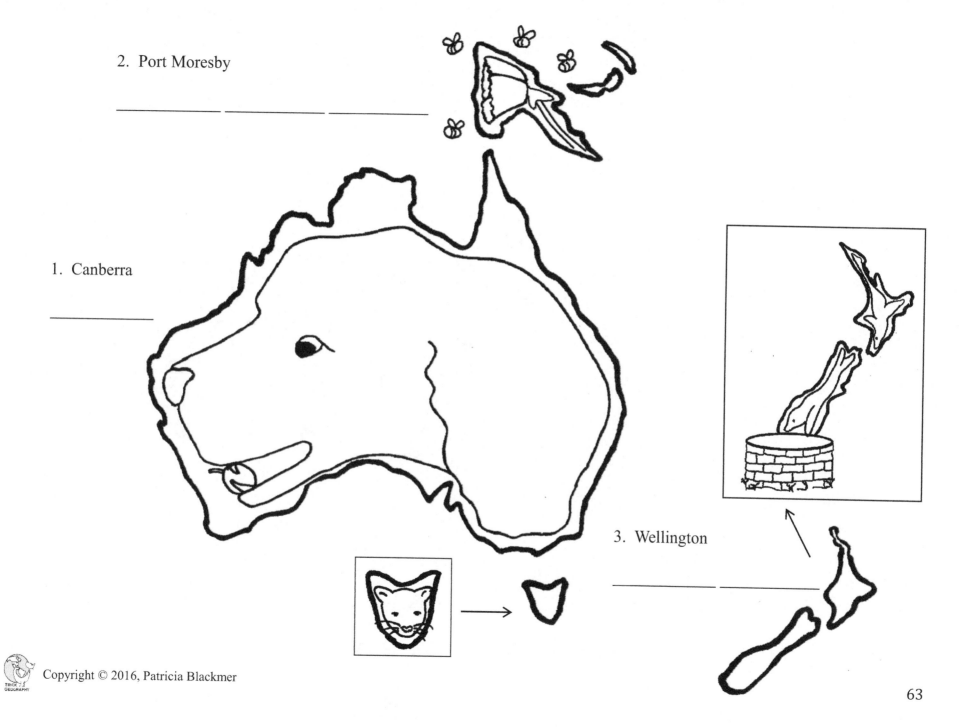

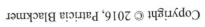

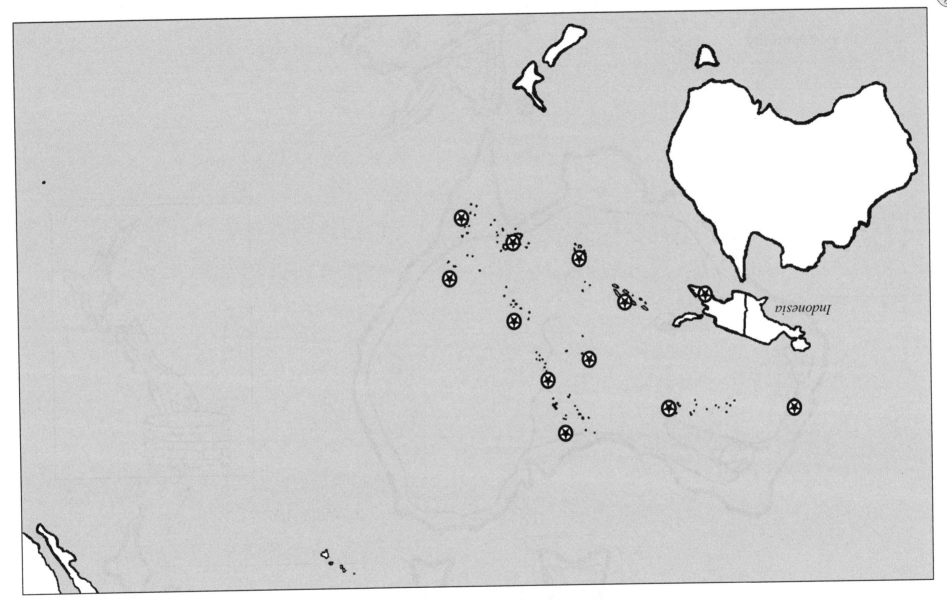

Indonesia

OCEANIA
MAP 5: PACIFIC ISLAND CAPITALS

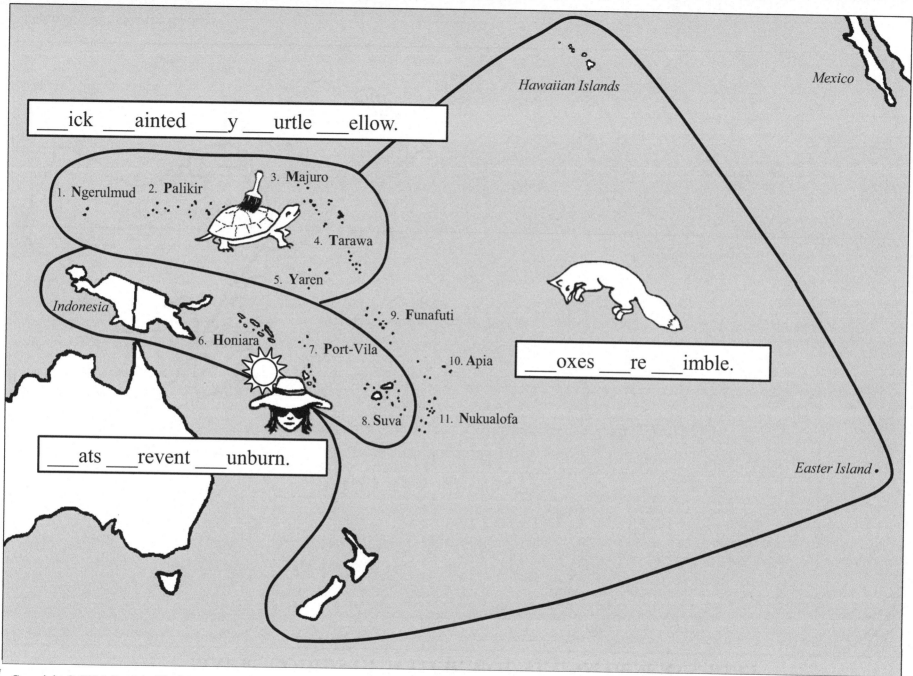

___ick ___ainted ___y ___urtle ___ellow.

Hawaiian Islands

Mexico

1. Ngerulmud 2. Palikir 3. Majuro

4. Tarawa

5. Yaren

Indonesia

9. Funafuti

6. Honiara 7. Port-Vila

10. Apia

___oxes ___re ___imble.

8. Suva 11. Nukualofa

___ats ___revent ___unburn.

Easter Island

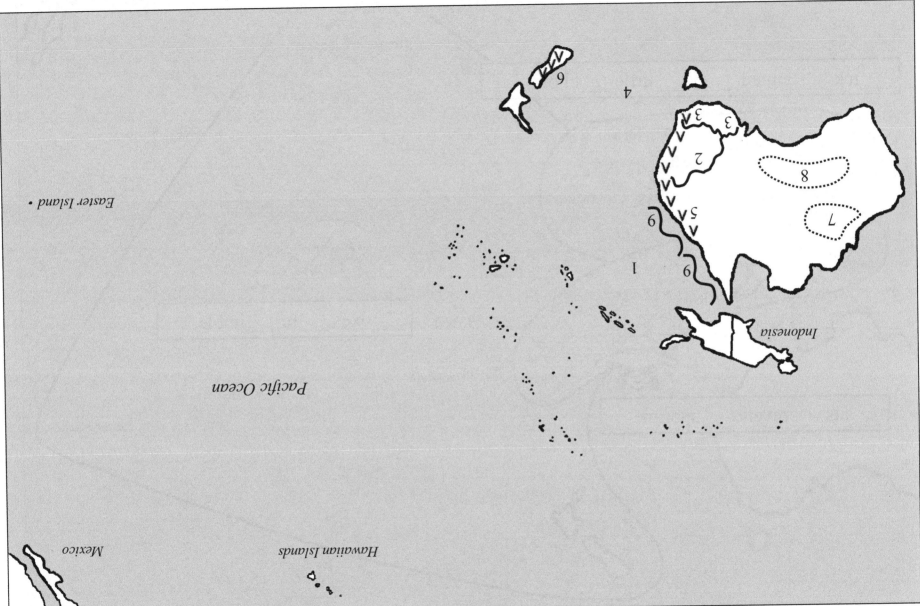

Easter Island •

Pacific Ocean

Mexico

Hawaiian Islands

Indonesia

OCEANIA

MAP 6: BODIES OF WATER, MOUNTAINS, DESERTS, REEF

Bodies of Water

1. **Coral** Sea: Poppies (Papua New Guinea) are red, not _____.

2. **Darling** River: A stray named Leah (Australia) is a _____ dog.

3. **Murray** River: A stray named Leah (Australia) is in a _____.

4. **Tasman** Sea: Lies east of _____.

Mountains

5. **Great Dividing** Range: A stray named Leah (Australia) can't _____ numbers.

6. **Southern Alps**: Two seals (New Zealand) swim _____ of the _____.

Deserts

7. **Great Sandy** Desert: A stray named Leah (Australia) has _____ paws.

8. **Great Victorian** Desert: _____ _____ fed a stray named Leah (Australia).

Reef

9. **Great Barrier** Reef: A stray named Leah (Australia) is behind a _____ _____.

No individual has any right to come into the world and go out of it without leaving behind him distinct and legitimate reasons for having passed through it.

—George Washington Carver

TESTS

UNIT 1: NORTH AMERICAN TESTS

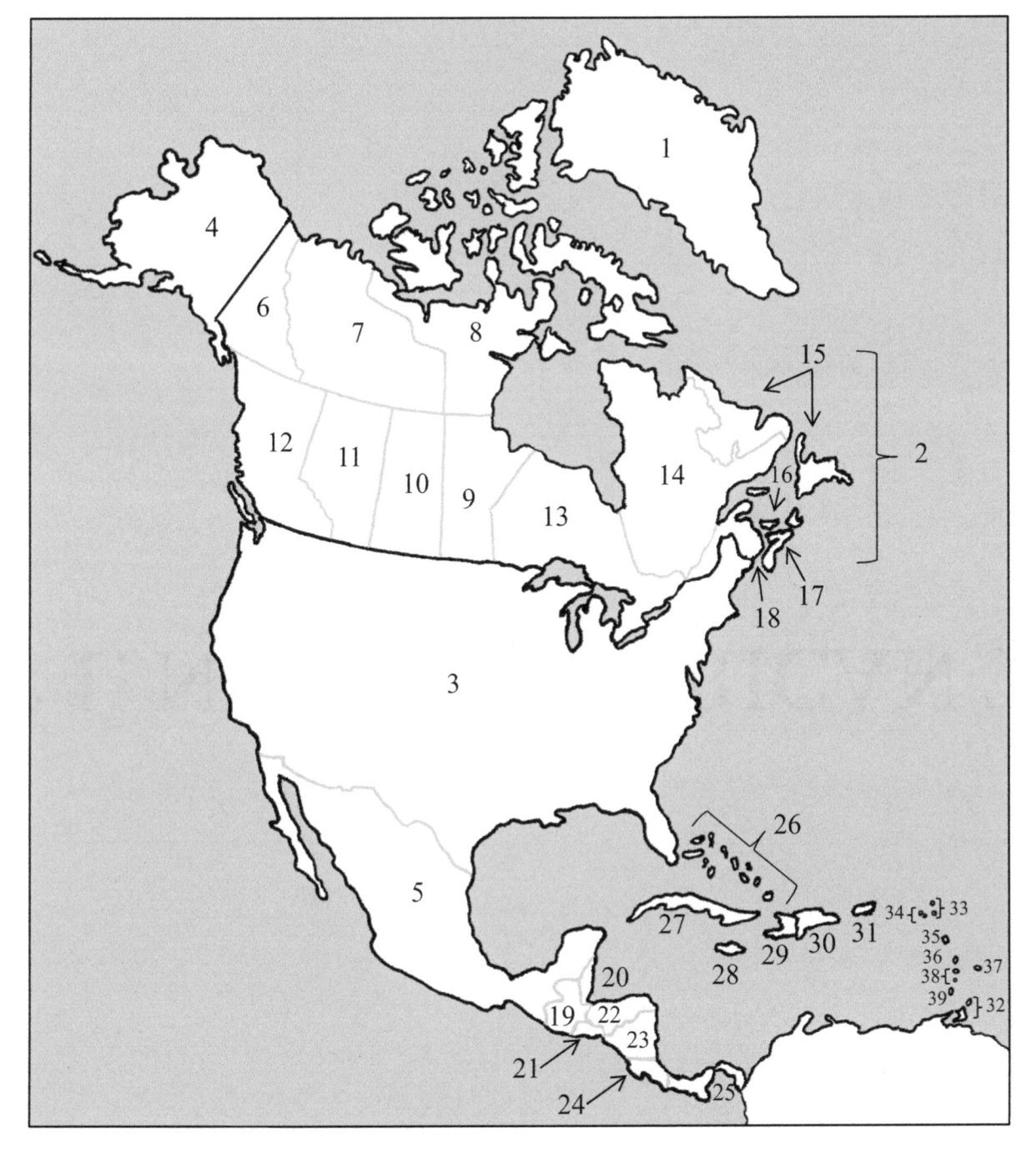

NORTH AMERICAN COUNTRIES, PROVINCES, TERRITORIES

Match the correct country, province, or territory with its number on the page above.

1. _____	21. _____	A. Alaska (USA)	U. Northwest Territories
2. _____	22. _____	B. Alberta	V. Nova Scotia
3. _____	23. _____	C. Bahamas	W. Nunavut
4. _____	24. _____	D. Belize	X. Ontario
5. _____	25. _____	E. British Columbia	Y. Panama
6. _____	26. _____	F. Canada	Z. Prince Edward Island
7. _____	27. _____	G. Costa Rica	AA. Puerto Rico
8. _____	28. _____	H. Cuba	BB. Quebec
9. _____	29. _____	I. Dominican Republic	CC. Saskatchewan
10. _____	30. _____	J. El Salvador	DD. Trinidad and Tobago
11. _____	31. _____	K. Greenland	EE. United States of America
12. _____	32. _____	L. Guatemala	FF. Yukon
13. _____		M. Haiti	
14. _____	**Islands:**	N. Honduras	**Islands:**
15. _____	33. _____	O. Jamaica	GG. Antiqua and Barbuda
16. _____	34. _____	P. Manitoba	HH. Barbados
17. _____	35. _____	Q. Mexico	II. Dominica
18. _____	36. _____	R. New Brunswick	JJ. Grenada
19. _____	37. _____	S. Newfoundland and Labrador	KK. St. Kitts and Nevis
20. _____	38. _____	T. Nicaragua	LL. St. Lucia
	39. _____		MM. St. Vincent and Grenadines

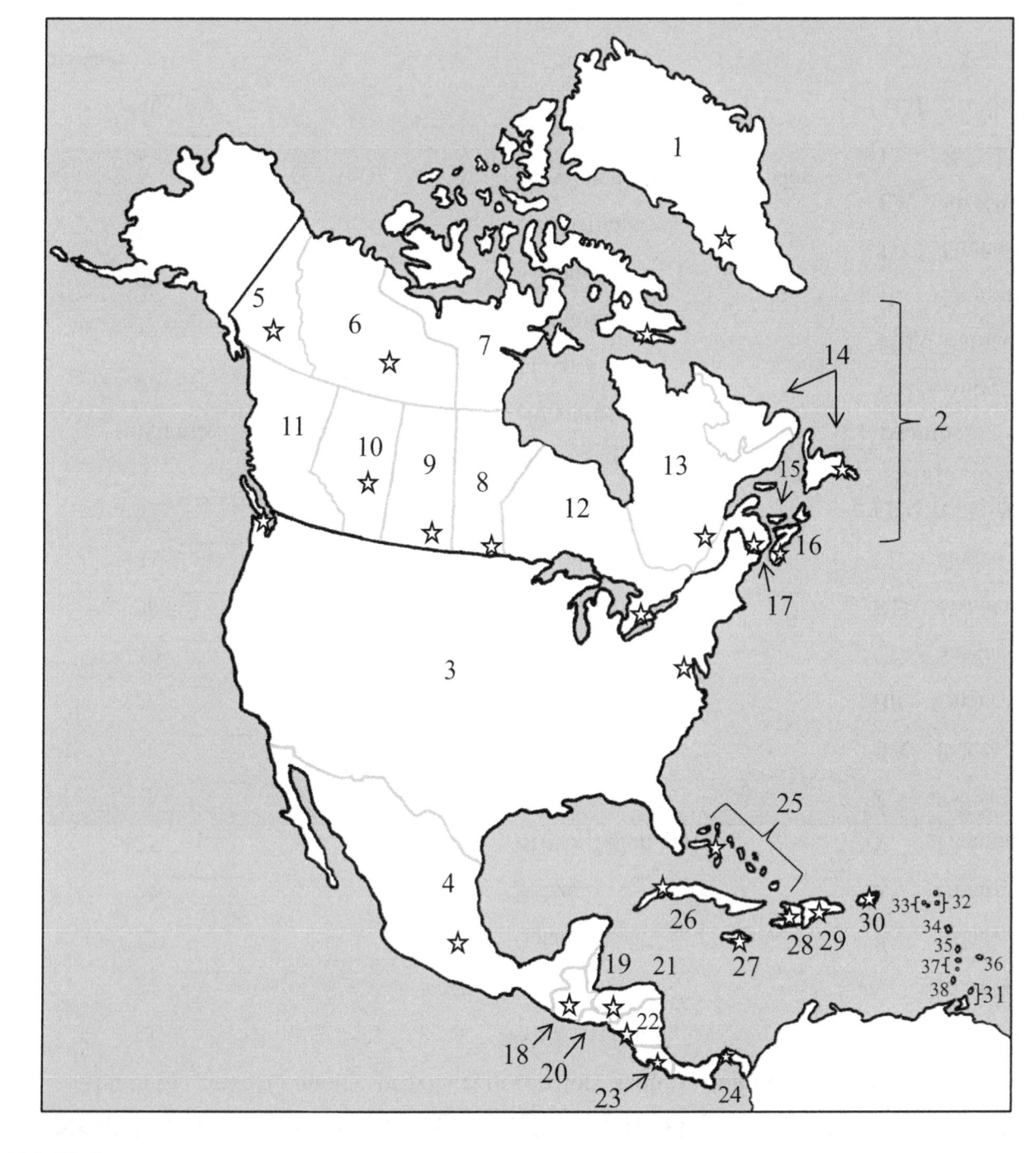

NORTH AMERICAN CAPITALS

Match the correct capital with its number on the page above.

1. _____	21. _____	
2. _____	22. _____	
3. _____	23. _____	
4. _____	24. _____	
5. _____	25. _____	
6. _____	26. _____	
7. _____	27. _____	
8. _____	28. _____	
9. _____	29. _____	
10. _____	30. _____	
11. _____	31. _____	
12. _____		
13. _____	**Islands:**	
14. _____	32. _____	
15. _____	33. _____	
16. _____	34. _____	
17. _____	35. _____	
18. _____	36. _____	
19. _____	37. _____	
20. _____	38. _____	

A.	Belmopan	U.	San Juan
B.	Charlottetown	V.	San Salvador
C.	Edmonton	W.	Santo Domingo
D.	Fredericton	X.	St. John
E.	Guatemala City	Y.	Tegucigalpa
F.	Halifax	Z.	Toronto
G.	Havana	AA.	Victoria
H.	Iqaluit	BB.	Washington, D.C.
I.	Kingston	CC.	Whitehorse
J.	Managua	DD.	Winnipeg
K.	Mexico City	EE.	Yellow Knife
L.	Nassau		
M.	Nuuk	**Islands:**	
N.	Ottawa	FF.	Basseterre
O.	Panama City	GG.	Bridgetown
P.	Port of Spain	HH.	Castries
Q.	Port-au-Prince	II.	Kingstown
R.	Quebec	JJ.	Roseau
S.	Regina	KK.	St. Georges
T.	San Jose	LL.	St. Johns

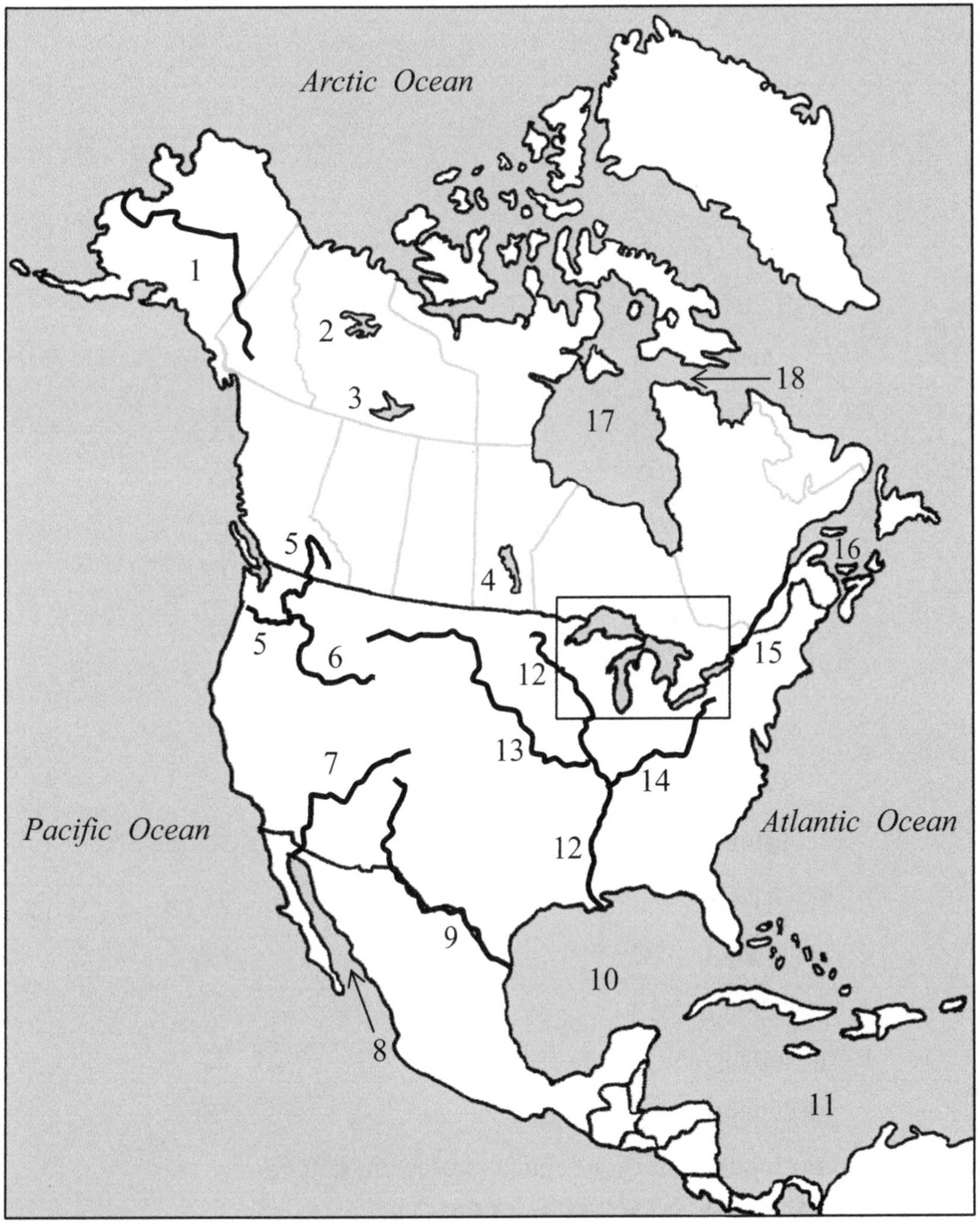

Arctic Ocean

1

2

3

18

17

5

4

16

5

6

12

15

13

14

7

12

Pacific Ocean

Atlantic Ocean

9

10

8

11

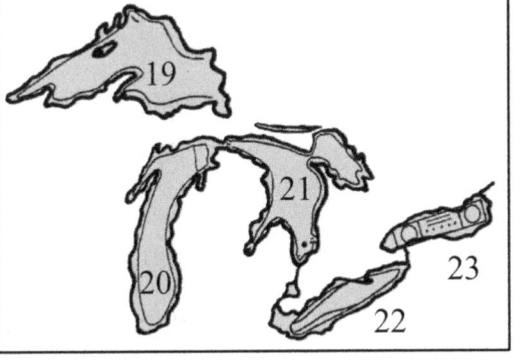

19

21

20

23

22

NORTH AMERICAN BODIES OF WATER

Match the correct body of water with its number on the page above.

1. _____   13. _____

2. _____   14. _____

3. _____   15. _____

4. _____   16. _____

5. _____   17. _____

6. _____   18. _____

7. _____   19. _____

8. _____   20. _____

9. _____   21. _____

10. _____   22. _____

11. _____   23. _____

12. _____

A.	Bear	M.	Missouri
B.	California	N.	Ohio
C.	Colorado	O.	Ontario
D.	Columbia	P.	Rio Grande
E.	Caribbean	Q.	Slave
F.	Erie	R.	Snake
G.	Hudson (bay)	S.	St. Lawrence (gulf)
H.	Hudson (strait)	T.	St. Lawrence (river)
I.	Huron	U.	Superior
J.	Mexico	V.	Winnipeg
K.	Michigan	W.	Yukon
L.	Mississippi		

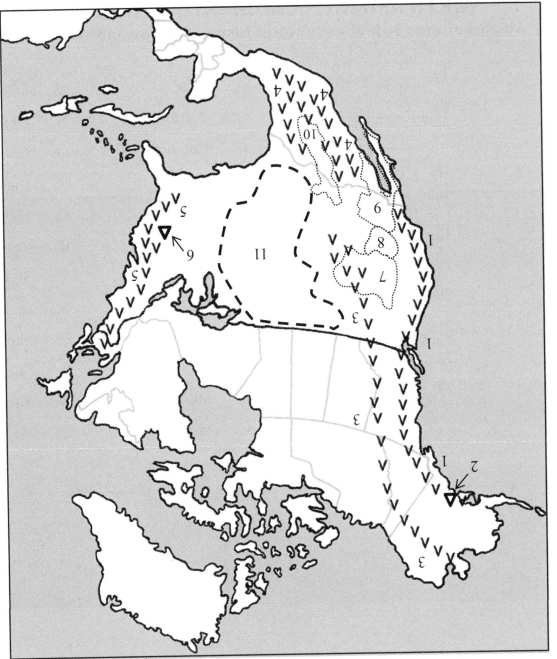

NORTH AMERICAN MOUNTAINS, DESERTS, PLAINS

Match the correct geographical feature with its number on the page above.

1. _____
2. _____
3. _____
4. _____
5. _____
6. _____
7. _____
8. _____
9. _____
10. _____
11. _____

A. Appalachian

B. Chihuahuan

C. Coastal

D. Denali (McKinley)

E. Great Basin

F. Great Plains

G. Mitchell

H. Mojave

I. Rocky

J. Sierra Madre

K. Sonoran

UNIT 2: SOUTH AMERICAN TESTS

SOUTH AMERICAN COUNTRIES, ISLANDS
Match the correct country with its number on the page above.

1. _____

2. _____

3. _____

4. _____

5. _____

6. _____

7. _____

8. _____

9. _____

10. _____

11. _____

12. _____

13. _____

14. _____

A. Argentina

B. Bolivia

C. Brazil

D. Chile

E. Columbia

F. Ecuador

G. French Guiana

H. Galapagos Islands

I. Guyana

J. Paraguay

K. Peru

L. Suriname

M. Uruguay

N. Venezuela

SOUTH AMERICN CAPITALS

Match the correct capital with its number on the page above.

1. _____		A.	Asuncion
2. _____		B.	Bogota
3. _____		C.	Brasilia
4. _____		D.	Buenos Aires
5. _____		E.	Caracas
6. _____		F.	Cayenne
7. _____		G.	Georgetown
8. _____		H.	La Pas
9. _____		I.	Lima
10. _____		J.	Montevideo
_____		K.	Paramaribo
11. _____		L.	Quito
12. _____		M.	Santiago
13. _____		N.	Sucre

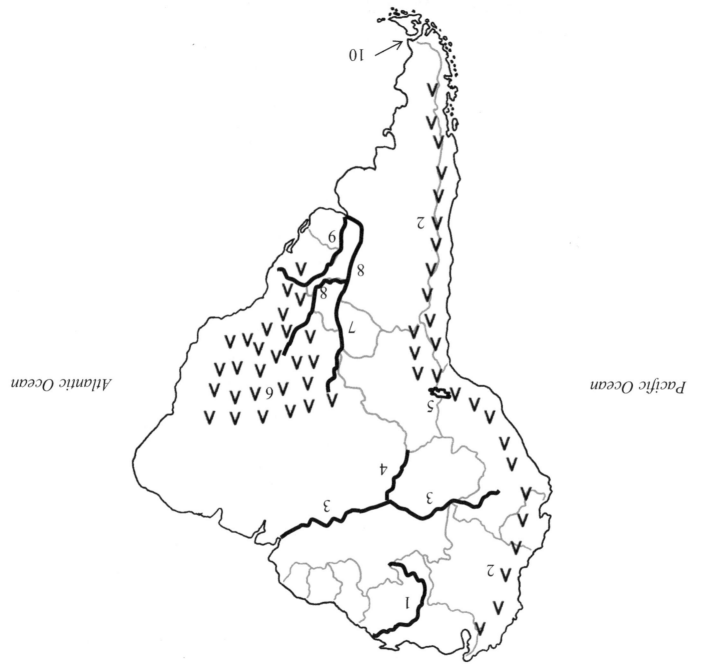

Pacific Ocean

Atlantic Ocean

SOUTH AMERICAN BODIES OF WATER, MOUNTAINS

Match the correct geographical feature with its number on the page above.

1. _____   A. Amazon

2. _____   B. Andes

3. _____   C. Brazilian Highlands

4. _____   D. Titicaca

5. _____   E. Madeira

6. _____   F. Orinoco

7. _____   G. Paraguay

8. _____   H. Paraná

9. _____   I. Magellan

10. _____   J. Uruguay

UNIT 3: OCEANIC TESTS

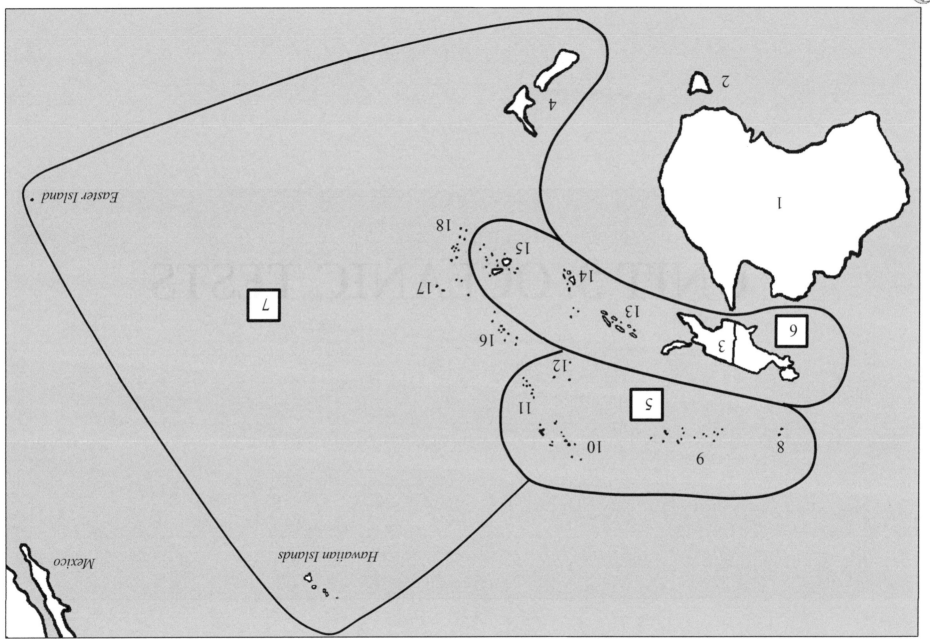

OCEANIC TESTS

Mexico

Hawaiian Islands

Easter Island

06

OCEANIC REGIONS, COUNTRIES, ISLANDS

Match the correct region, country, or island with its number on the page above.
(Region numbers appear inside boxes.)

1. _____		A.	Australia
2. _____		B.	Melanesia
3. _____		C.	Micronesia
4. _____		D.	New Zealand
5. _____		E.	Papua New Guinea
6. _____		F.	Polynesia
7. _____		G.	Tasmania

Small Islands: **Small Islands:**

8. _____		H.	Federated States of Micronesia
9. _____		I.	Fiji
10. _____		J.	Kiribati
11. _____		K.	Marshall Islands
12. _____		L.	Nauru
13. _____		M.	Palau
14. _____		N.	Samoa
15. _____		O.	Solomon Islands
16. _____		P.	Tonga
17. _____		Q.	Tuvalu
18. _____		R.	Vanuatu

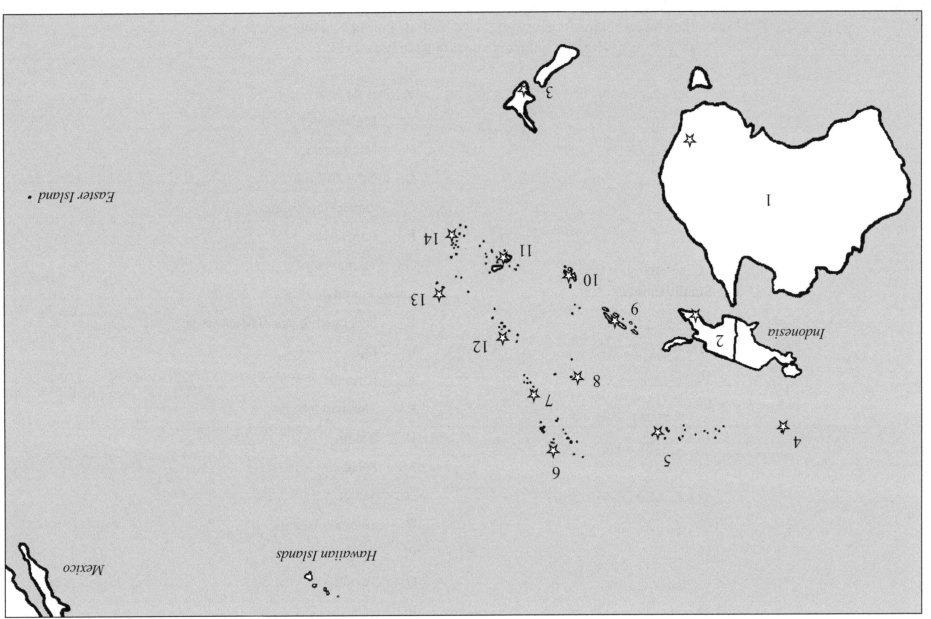

Easter Island

Mexico

Hawaiian Islands

Indonesia

OCEANIC CAPITALS

Match the correct capital with its number on the page above.

1. _____   A. Canberra

2. _____   B. Port Moresby

3. _____   C. Wellington

Small Islands: **Small Islands:**

4. _____   D. Apia

5. _____   E. Funafuti

6. _____   F. Honiara

7. _____   G. Majuro

8. _____   H. Ngerulmud

9. _____   I. Nukualofa

10. _____   J. Palikir

11. _____   K. Port-Vila

12. _____   L. Suva

13. _____   M. Tarawa

14. _____   N. Yaren

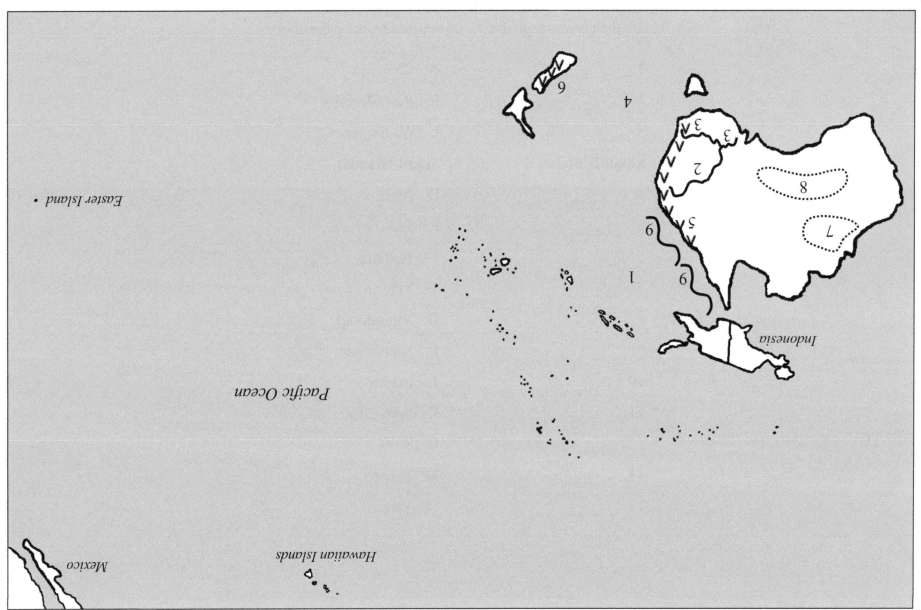

Easter Island •

Pacific Ocean

Mexico

Hawaiian Islands

Indonesia

OCEANIC BODIES OF WATER, MOUNTAINS, DESERTS, REEF

Match the correct physical feature with its number on the page above.

1. _____   A. Coral

2. _____   B. Darling

3. _____   C. Great Barrier

4. _____   D. Great Dividing Range

5. _____   E. Great Sandy

6. _____   F. Great Victorian

7. _____   G. Murray

8. _____   H. Southern Alps

9. _____   I. Tasman

TRICK GEOGRAPHY®
Companion Series
The quick and simple way to geographic mastery!

"I can't believe how much I just learned!" That was one mom's response after observing a single class session of *Trick Geography*.

Trick Geography routinely moves students from geographic illiteracy to command of world countries and US states with ease and high retention. It also teaches world and US capitals and major bodies of water, mountains, peninsulas, and deserts.

Delightful graphics, phonetic connectors, dot-to-dots, and fill-in-the-blanks facilitate multiple learning styles. The process is more like a game than a curriculum. While *Trick Geography* is easy enough for elementary students, it is sophisticated enough for the high schooler.

Teachers appreciate the simple instructions which require virtually no prep time and which give students the option of going through the program on their own. Pronunciation guides for many names expedite the teaching process as well.

Evaluation is a cinch with matching tests.

Trick Geography: USA

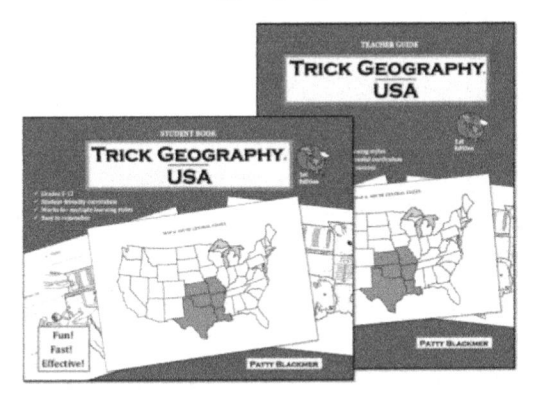

Trick Geography: World

Wholesalers contact Trick Geography for quantity discounts at:
TrickGeography@outlook.com

Made in the USA
Monee, IL
25 August 2021